ANYTHING IS PAWSIBLE

IMPOSSIBLE DOG DREAMS COME TRUE

by

Tes M. Kurtz

Photographs by Andy Sheng

A collection of true, inspiring
short stories about rescued dogs

ACKNOWLEDGMENTS

Thank you, Jennie Wong, for all your help jumpstarting this important project.

Thank you, Anything Is PAWSible family, for sharing your adoption and
rescue stories. You make a profound and positive difference in the world.
I am in awe of each and every one of you.

Thank you, Aunt Nese, for Purses for Pooches.
Your belief and support of the publication of *Anything Is PAWSible* made all the difference.

Thank you, Michelle Bowles, for dedicating your time and talent. You are a stellar editor.

Thank you, Ryan Jacobson, for your publishing guidance and layout expertise.

Thank you, Vanessa Mendozzi, for designing a stunning book cover.

DEDICATIONS

To Filbert, Monroe, Chance, Parker and Pinot,
Forever in my heart.

To all the homeless animals around the world,
May each and every one of your dreams of comfort, love and a forever home come true.

To my Landmark family
Especially,
Tim
We are all connected in this world of infinite possibilities. Thank you for the gift.

And, my Self Expression Leadership Program (SELP) besties,
Joel, Brooke, David, Danielle, Chema
This is it. And, it's perfect.

To my family and friends,
Thank you for your patience.
Thank you for your understanding.
Thank you for helping me make my own dream come true.

TABLE OF CONTENTS

Impossible Dog Dreams Come True

1. Being Inspired to Adopt Is PAWSible 7

2. Adopting a Pure Breed or Designer Crossbreed from the Shelter Is PAWSible 16

3. Changing a Heart Is PAWSible 21

4. Adopting a Senior Dog Is PAWSible 27

5. Interconnectedness Is PAWSible 34

6. Opening Your Heart to Love Again Is PAWSible 42

7. Big Hearts Growing Bigger Is PAWSible 45

8. Bad Luck Turning Into Good Luck Is PAWSible 51

9. Rags to Riches Is PAWSible 56

10. A Guardian Angel Is PAWSible 64

11. Stopping Abuse and Neglect Is PAWSible 69

12. Paying Love and Kindness Forward Is PAWSible 76

13. Taking a Stand for Animals Is PAWSible 82

14. Dedicating Your Life to Serving Animals and Your Community Is PAWSible 87

15. Receiving an Unexpected Gift Is PAWSible 102

16. Volunteering for an Animal Shelter or Rescue Is PAWSible 110

Cats Have Paws, Too

17. Surviving Against the Odds Is PAWSible 115

18-1. Supporting Cat Rescues Is PAWSible 118

18-2. Becoming A Certified Therapy Dog Is PAWSible 121

18-3. Trap, Neuter, Release Is PAWSible 126

18-4. Honoring A Furry Friend Is PAWSible 130

19. Becoming Master of a Human Is PAWSible 135

20. Fostering Is PAWSible 137

Rabbits Have Paws, Too

21-1. Creating a Bunny Sanctuary Is PAWSible 147

21-2. Saving Show Rabbits Is PAWSible 149

21-3. Bonding With A Bunny Is PAWSible 151

21-4. A Genius Bunny Is PAWSible 153

21-5. Foster Failing Is PAWSible 156

21-6. A Surprise Is PAWSible 158

22. Making Animals a Priority in Your Community Is PAWSible 160

23. Being a Hero Is PAWSible 165

Sources 169

IMPOSSIBLE DOG
DREAMS COME TRUE

1

BEING INSPIRED TO ADOPT IS PAWSIBLE

Animals fascinate me. I've always felt a special connection to them. It's hard to explain. It's a feeling. An understanding. Respect. I have a vague memory of the first time I saw a dog. Mostly, it's an image ingrained in my head from the story my mom tells me. I was a toddler bundled from head to toe—crocheted hat with a ball on top and matching mittens-on-a-string knitted by my grandmother, insolated rubber boots and a 1970s brown parka with a fuzz-trimmed hood—to keep my just-started-walking self sheltered from the tundra of North Dakota. My mom was holding my hand and a dog as big as me walked by us on a leash with his human. Mesmerized, my big blue eyes grew extra large as I stared in awe at this delightful creature.

As I grew, I got to know a few dogs up close and personal. My aunt had a cool Border Collie mix named Max. They lived in a small Minnesota town where he was constantly going on adventures and getting into mischief. My cousins had a cuddly Poodle mix named Muffy. She was more of a homebody but did go on some family road trips—visiting relatives, camping. I loved them both and dreamed of having a dog of my own.

When I was nine years old, I watched *Old Yeller* on TV for the first (and last) time. I was transfixed and fell in love with that yellow dog. The ending traumatized me. I cried for days. I wanted to fix him. I wanted to make Old Yeller all better and change the ending of his story. I still do.

Soon after my childhood world lost Old Yeller to rabies, my bedroom became a veterinary office. The patients were my collection of stuffed animals. The hallway was the waiting room. Piggy, Holly Hobby, Benji, Pooh, Eeyore, Colby the Dog, Fluffy the Bear, and the rest of the fuzzy masses lined up to be tended to by a young girl determined to save them all. One by one, I called them into the examination room for a check-up. Some were treated with hydrogen peroxide and a bandage to heal their wounds; others got the thumbs up and an adoring hug. Once in a while, I had to perform surgery. A stitch here. A stitch there. Never any fatalities.

About this same time, I started begging my parents for a dog. They eventually gave in when my dad's co-worker was looking for a new home for his elderly mother's Maltese-Pekingese mix. The woman's deteriorating health prevented her from taking care of four-year-old Fluffy.

The first thing Fluffy did when she met us was show off her best tricks. She effortlessly sprung straight in the air as high as the kitchen counter and then sat eagerly waiting for a treat. She was a long-haired, white jumping bean with an underbite. The girl also had some dance moves. She stood on her hind legs and twirled 'round and 'round. I fell in love instantly. She made me giggle.

I adoringly coddled her. Fluffy was with us for nearly four years until she got out one day and never came back. I was devastated. I do not know the ending of her story. My heart never mended from losing her.

We didn't have another family dog. I finished high school and college. I graduated from the University of North Dakota in December and had plans to move to Colorado in February. Shortly after graduation, my friends and I were at our favorite hangout, Bonzer's Pub. They served schooners of beer and delivered endless free baskets of unshelled peanuts. By the end of most nights, the bar floor was varying degrees of sticky and layered in peanut shells.

Since it was the holidays, the establishment staff jazzed things up a bit and served mixed holiday nuts in the baskets. As I fantasized out loud about what life in Denver would be like as a young adult, I reached into the basket of nuts and pulled out a small, round, brown one that I had never seen before.

"What kind of nut is this?"

"I think that's a filbert nut." My friend, Ellen, was quick to know her nuts.

"A what?"

"A filbert nut."

"Filbert?"

"Yah. F-I-L-B-E-R-T. Filbert."

The name tickled me pink. It induced a laughter so hearty that my gut ached and I snorted uncontrollably, like Chrissy Snow on *Three's Company*.

"I'm going to move to Denver and get a dog and name him Filbert!"

I declared it. I did it.

Four years later, I went through a break up. The only remedy for my broken heart was the dog I had spent years longing for. It was time. I needed to find my Filbert.

This is part of my pathway to dog rescue that many animal advocates and dog rescuers may not like. I ask you to bear with me. Life is a journey of lessons, and this was the beginning of mine. My hope is that by sharing my stories and the stories of others, I will open the door to the world of dog rescue and adoption—just as Filbert opened the door for me.

Here's my confession:

I went to the pet store. In the mall. To buy Filbert.

There were and are a few big problems associated with this choice. I will get to those soon.

When I entered the pet store, there were adorable puppies everywhere. All pure breeds. A Shih Tzu caught my eye. He was a cute fuzz ball. I held him, but didn't feel a connection. My yearning for a connection with him far outweighed our chemistry.

Soon after I held the wee one, another woman held him. They connected. I saw it and was envious. None of the other puppies in the windows "spoke" to me. I decided it just wasn't meant to be for me that day. With my head bowed down and shoulders slumped forward in disappointment, I exited the store. As I did, an adorable, tiny something curled up in a ball in the corner of the store front display window caught my eye. I stopped in my tracks and turned to get a close, direct look. I knew instantly. Filbert!

I rushed back in the store and approached the sales lady. "Can I meet that doggy in the window?"

She brought him to me, and he rested his head perfectly satisfied on my shoulder. It felt like home.

"What kind of dog is he?"

"He's a white and lemon Papillon."

"How old?"

"Three months."

"His ears are HUGE! How big will he get?"

She laughed at my observation. "Papillon means 'butterfly' in French. They are known for their large, butterfly-like ears. He should grow into them a little bit, but Papillons don't get very big. Maybe 15 pounds at the most. They are a perfect apartment dog."

"How much does he cost?"

"He is a purebred Papillon and comes with papers. He's $480."

It all sounded so important. What did it mean?

The sales person showed me the very important papers. It was a Certificate of Registration with an official seal of the Continental Kennel Club (CKC). The name listed for the dam was "Tess's She's-A-Inspiration"—the breeder name followed by the doggy mom name. Although spelled differently, the breeder and I shared the same first name. It was a sign from the universe that confirmed what I already felt. This little guy and I belonged together.

So, I bought Filbert from the pet store in the mall. All two and a half pounds of him.

I never submitted the transfer of ownership paperwork to the CKC. It didn't mean anything to me. I wasn't his "owner." I was his mom. We were family.

I did do the important things. I licensed Filbert with the city. Kept him up to date on all his shots. Attached current dog tags with my contact information on his collar. If microchipping was available at that time, I would have done it. I cared for him. Trained him. Took him everywhere. Loved him as a mother loves a child. Filbert wanted for nothing. He never knew life on the streets. He never experienced abandonment. He was never abused. He never went hungry. He never knew a cold cement floor of a shelter. My future dogs would, but Filbert only knew safety, comfort, and love. His entire long life.

My little nut lived up to his name. Filbert was funny and surprisingly athletic for a dainty dude, who never reached more than seven pounds. He loved hiking. His favorite toy to play fetch with was a headless frog—he chewed off the rubber head as a puppy. Each night, Filbert slept curled around my head. It was like wearing a Russian ushanka-hat to bed.

Every day when I returned home from work, my Happy Papi greeted me with a wagging curled tail. When I asked, "How was your day, Fil-B?" He answered in an animated, conversational gurgle. Some stories were short and sweet. Some were long and detailed. He was a grand storyteller.

He had another unique talent. When Filbert peed, he performed a walking handstand. It was quite a sight. I had a neighbor who was so amazed and amused by this "trick" that she made a point to come out for Filbert's "show" every day when I took him for his late afternoon walks.

Filbert and I walked a lot. When you take your dog for walks, you bump into other people walking their dogs. Conversations start as your dogs sniff each other's butts and get acquainted. You learn stuff. The more I learned, the more I researched. Here are the most important lessons that Filbert helped me learn:

1. I was likely supporting puppy mills when I purchased Filbert from the pet store in the mall. I'm ashamed of that. Most pet store puppies come from puppy mills, which are dog-breeding facilities. Conditions are deplorable. Imagine spending your entire life confined to a small wire cage with barely enough room to turn around. This is the horrifying life of most dogs in puppy mills. They don't know what grass beneath their paws feels like. They are unnecessarily punished slaves that do without. Without food and water. Without freedom to run and play. Without human affection. Without veterinary care.

These abused and neglected dogs are usually bred over and over and over again. When they can no longer produce, they are thrown out like trash or killed.

I do not know for certain whether Filbert's mom and dad were puppy mill dogs. What I do know is that the pet store from which I purchased Filbert in 1995 is still in the Denver area. Recent public reviews and Better Business Bureau complaints point out serious behavioral and health issues of puppies purchased there. One reviewer even traced the registration paperwork of her purchased dog to one of the top 100 worst puppy mills in the country as listed by the Humane Society of the United States (HSUS).

2. Official registration papers don't mean anything. Not to me. Not to anyone who just wants to provide a loveable dog a happy, loving home. What does mean something are the good treatment and well-being of our animals.

HSUS points out, "Purebred 'papers' don't tell you anything about where a puppy was raised or how her parents were treated." That is exactly the case with Filbert. How his parents were treated by their breeders was not revealed to me and remains unknown. I own that failure to investigate and dig deeper.

The truth is that the American Kennel Club (AKC) often fights laws that fight puppy mills. A 2012 report published by HSUS revealed "the AKC had opposed more than 80 different laws around the country that would protect dogs from puppy mills. Since then, that number has climbed to more than 150."

In addition to fighting puppy mill laws, the AKC, along with the CKC, supports one of the largest puppy mill organizations in the world, Missouri Pet Breeders Association. Both are listed on the organization's website as platinum donation supporters.

It's all about the money. Canine registration services are supported by the registration fees that breeders pay. The more puppies that breeders register, the more money for that dog registry.

If you do choose to buy from a breeder, be sure to visit the facility so you can see the conditions where the dogs are being raised. Better yet, don't buy at all. Adopt! Go to your nearest animal shelter or reach out to your favorite dog rescue organization.

3. A purebred dog does not mean a better dog. Breeding dogs all started with the human desire to create perfect looking dogs with predictable behavior. The problem is that nowadays the gene pool for registries, like the AKC, is limited. They only allow breeding of dogs within their registry. So, a gene pool that started 130 years ago with 50 dogs is now a gene pool where most dogs are related. Cousins mating with cousins. In today's world, most purebred dogs are inbred dogs. The results are dogs that may look perfect on the outside, but are highly vulnerable to genetic diseases.

4. Spaying and neutering saves lives in two important ways:

Helping prevent unnecessary euthanasia due to overcrowding in shelters; and

Saving or prolonging your own dog or cat's life

Every year, six to eight million healthy animals enter shelters. Only about half get adopted. The rest are unnecessarily euthanized to make room for more homeless animals. That's four million healthy, viable, home-worthy dogs and cats killed because of overcrowded shelters. Spaying and neutering helps control the pet population.

Spaying and neutering may also help your own dog live a longer, healthier life. Spaying female dogs reduces the chances of her developing a fatal uterine infection, uterine cancer, and other cancers of the reproductive system. She also won't go into heat. That means no lusty mating calls or urinating in the house in an effort to attract a male from the neighborhood for a booty call.

Neutering males eliminates any chance of them getting testicular cancer, and may reduce chances of getting prostate cancer. It certainly reduces their urge to roam the neighborhood in search of finding a female in heat so he can "plant his seed". When unneutered males venture out in search of a female to mount, they also increase their chances of injury or death—getting hit by a car, getting into fights with other animals. Anything can happen when animals decide to hit the road and explore on their own.

There are other benefits to spaying and neutering. Your dog will calm down a notch or two. They are less likely to display bad habits like excessive barking, mounting, urine-marking and other dominance-related behaviors.

In the long run, you will also save money. There are low-cost spay/neuter clinics available in most communities across the country. The small, one-time expense to spay or neuter is far, far, far less than any medical costs you could face if your pet acquires an illness related to keeping their reproductive organs intact.

As an added bonus, renewing pet licenses for spayed/neutered pets can be less expensive. More and more communities are requiring sterilized pets. If your pet is not, you may pay an extra fee for pet license renewal.

5. Adopting saves lives. If you adopt from a local shelter or rescue organization, you actually save two lives: the life of the dog you adopt, and the life of the dog who gets to take your new family member's spot in the shelter or rescue.

There are hundreds of reasons and situations why amazing dogs end up in shelters. None of them are any fault of their own. As humans, we domesticated these animals. It is our job to care for them. Treat them with respect. Be kind. Be responsible for them.

Shelters offer choices galore. Pure breeds, designer cross breeds, mutts; puppies, seniors, and every age in between. If you have your heart set on a specific purebred or crossbred dog, you can find one at your local animal shelter, or go directly to a rescue organization that specializes in saving and adopting out specific breeds. The one your heart is looking for is ready and waiting for you.

You will never regret adopting and saving a life. I know I haven't.

A year and a half after buying Filbert from a pet store, I adopted Monroe from Denver Dumb Friends League Animal Shelter. I learned my lesson. I wanted to save a life.

On March 10, 1997, Filbert and I met a dog named Rover. I paid $65 to add a six-month-old Basenji mix to my family. That fee included having him neutered and up to date on shots. On March 11th, I brought him home and bestowed him a name befitting his regal elegance. Monroe.

Everyone who met Monroe loved him. He was a cool, cool dog. A typical Basenji, he did not bark. However, strange noises did make their way out of his mouth. He didn't speak often, but when he did, you had no choice but to listen.

Monroe spoke "Shyriiwook" fluently—he sounded exactly like Chewbacca from Star Wars. It was a boisterous noise that provoked endless double-take looks and startled jumps. When people realized it was coming from a 35-pound harmless sweetheart, grins emerged and chuckles ensued. He prompted more curious looks when ambulances, fire trucks, or police cars whizzed through the neighborhood. The blaring sirens put Monroe to a halt. He belted out a unique, laborious, yodel-sounding howl that put any Bloodhound or Beagle to shame.

'Roe had an extreme talent for hunting. This city dog was fascinating to watch when he spotted a pigeon or squirrel. He was quick to crouch low with his head and neck extended forward, and front right paw bent, pointing toward his prey. Motionless. Focused. Waiting. He was oblivious to my voice or any other surrounding sounds.

If Monroe was on a leash when he was in the hunting zone, I made sure to hold on extra tight and be ready to sprint, or just let go of it completely. When the moment was right, he flew like lightning toward his prey. No warning. No flinching. Instantaneous.

Squirrels always made it to the safety of a tree or fence top, leaving Monroe bewildered by their ability to outsmart and outrun him. Fixated, he sat at the bottom of the tree or fence on which they were perched as they taunted him. "Nah-nah-nah, boo-boo. You can 't catch us!" He yodeled and yodeled and yodeled in great frustration. Pigeons were another story. They weren't always as quick as the squirrels. They usually got away. Usually. I must admit to a few casualties.

Monroe was an independent spirit. I took him to enclosed parks often, so he could explore free of a leash. Watching him run fast and free in an open field was breathtaking. He was pure grace. His elation and appreciation were evident by the huge smile he wore on his face.

'Roe and I went rollerblading together from time to time along the Cherry Creek bike path in Denver. It was a smooth and wide cemented trail—perfect for rollerblading with a canine friend. There were two ways to get to the bike path along city streets from my place on Capitol Hill: A short direct route down a steep grade; or a longer, roundabout way on flatter streets.

I once made the poor choice of taking the short, steep route. We started off going carefully down the sharply slanted sidewalk, and made it halfway down. Then, Monroe spotted a squirrel. He bolted. I was able to hang on for a block, but he was too fast. His leash slipped out of my hands, and I fell flat on my ass. Terrified he would be hit by a car, I got up quickly and bladed after him yelling," Monroe! Stop! Roe! Wait!" Ever so focused, he kept racing toward the squirrel. I held my breath and prayed as he crossed a major street.

A tree saved the day. The squirrel ran up it. Monroe planted himself at the bottom of it. As he pleaded with the squirrel to come back down, I grabbed hold of his leash, caught my breath, and thanked God. We never took that route to the bike path again.

Obviously, Monroe, the hunter, had an extra bit of energy to expend. In addition to random rollerblading outings, he and I went on a couple of runs without Filbert during the week. But Filbert joined us for all of our walking and hiking adventures. They both loved hiking.

Filbert and Monroe were great buddies. They shared many personality traits and interests that made living together fun and peaceful. Both were highly alert and energetic; friendly, intelligent, playful and affectionate.

We had a quirky morning ritual. When I blow dried my hair, I bent over at the waist and flipped my hair upside down to dry the underside first. Just like Pavlov's bell, the sound of the hair dryer turning on brought both of my boys running to sit at my feet. As I dried my hair with one hand, they received loving pets and scratches with the other. This happened every single day.

They did have some distinct differences. My Happy Papi was a cheerful fella. He loved everyone, but had a keen instinct for danger. I learned to listen to his highly intuitive nature quickly. He was methodical and obsessive-compulsive. At eating time, he took two pellets of dry dog food from his bowl in the kitchen, carried them to a corner in the living room, and gently laid them on the carpet. When he finished chewing each pellet one at a time, he would walk back to his bowl, take two more, return to the same spot on the carpet, and repeat, repeat, repeat until full.

Monroe was aloof to strangers but affectionate to those he knew and came to love. He enjoyed sitting on the couch and would lift one of his front paws for the human sitting next to him to hold. He loved to sit and hold hands.

The greatest difference between Filbert and Monroe was that Monroe possessed an innate appreciation for life and for me that Filbert lacked. Filbert adored me and was attached to me like glue, but Monroe had survived the streets. He knew how it felt to go hungry. He knew how it felt to be homeless. He knew he was saved. There is something to be said for adopting or rescuing a dog. They know. And, they never forget.

Despite the fact that both of these beautiful boys came into my life in different ways, they were both my family. Forever. They depended on me. I took care of them and loved them, but I think they gave me more.

They were there for me through good times and bad times during half of my 20s and most of my 30s. They were advisers during adventures of dating. These dogs stayed by my side through the highs of an engagement and the lows of a brief, tumultuous marriage. They supported me emotionally through a separation and move to California.

Just before my divorce was final, the dogs and I went on a walk with the man who would soon no longer be part of our lives. We sat in the grass at the park together. Filbert was in my lap. Monroe was antsy and kept eyeing this sitting man who had been part of his pack for the last three years. With deliberate intentions, Monroe walked behind the guy, lifted his leg, and peed on his back. I'm not sure who felt more satisfaction from his rebellious act of territory marking—him or me. It might be me.

Filbert and Monroe continued to be there for me as I enjoyed the triumphs of winning new jobs and buying my first home. They cheered me on as I re-entered the world of dating. Fil-B and 'Roe stuck by my side through the lows of fighting serious physical illness and battling chronic depression. There were lows so low, moments of such deep hopelessness, that the only reason I am still here is thanks to the two beautiful pairs of eyes watching over me and loving me without judgment. I owe my life to Filbert and Monroe.

Dogs are amazing no matter how you cut it. It seems whatever you give them in the way of love and care, they give back tenfold. Filbert and Monroe taught me the immeasurable value of an animal's life. Every single animal is worth saving. Every single animal deserves to know comfort, love and joy.

With the millions of dogs, cats and rabbits that are out in the world homeless, I hope the stories you are about to read will inspire you to adopt and welcome at least one, maybe two or three or more, into your home. If you are considering adding a dog, cat, rabbit, or even a turtle to your family, adopting is the kindest, wisest, most heroic option available.

2

ADOPTING A PURE BREED OR DESIGNER CROSSBREED FROM THE SHELTER IS PAWSIBLE

Together for many years, Alaina and her boyfriend, Matthew, wanted a dog. The timing was never quite right. Their hectic work schedules didn't allow them the time they felt they needed to devote to a dog. A fortunate turn of events changed that. Matthew started working from home. This dog-loving duo excitedly agreed it was finally the right time to bring a furry friend into their family. The couple also agreed to adopt from a shelter.

Alaina had one important requirement. She wanted a dog that was hypoallergenic and did not shed. Entertaining at home was one of Alaina's greatest joys. Since she had near and dear friends with allergies, she wanted a dog that could be part of any get-togethers that she and Matthew hosted without worry that someone she cared about would have an allergic reaction to their new family member. Alaina hated the thought of having to tuck their new pup alone in a room whenever company came over.

A friend of Alaina's, who was involved in the world of pet rescue and adoption, shared a link to a dog that fit the bill. The dog had medical issues that they could manage, and was located at the Lancaster shelter in northern Los Angeles County. They drove north to the shelter to meet the dog. When they arrived, the dog was already adopted.

"I guess it just wasn't meant to be," Matthew consoled his disappointed girlfriend. They looked around the shelter for another dog that would fit into their family, but none were quite right.

"Matt, there are plenty of shelters. We can check them all if we have to. It would be worth it to find the perfect match and save a life." Alaina and Matthew mapped out four other shelters in the northern part of Los Angeles County, and then hit the road determined to find their perfect canine companion.

"You ready for this?" Matthew was concerned the search they were about to embark on would be pretty tough emotionally—for both of them.

"Yes, I'm ready. We just can't bring home an entire farmhouse!" Alaina joked. She and Matthew both knew that they were going to want to adopt every dog they saw.

As they walked through the endless rows of kennels inside shelter after shelter, there was no denying the heartbreak of it all. So many dogs needing homes. Hundreds of pairs of pleading eyes watching them in hopes of being picked. Desperate barks pierced their eardrums, each of them begging, "Please get me out of here and bring me home. Please love me."

"You doin' alright?" Matthew was asking himself just as much as he was asking Alaina. In fact, he was impressed by how focused his girlfriend was staying. She knew what she wanted.

After walking through the fourth shelter, they were ready to give up. "I don't know how much more I can take, Matthew! We're close to Magic Mountain. Let's just ride roller coasters the rest of the day."

They both mulled over the fun diversion for a moment, and then realized how much they truly wanted a furry friend to love. Saving a life far outweighed the split-second notion of spending the rest of the day at an amusement park.

They stuck to their endeavor with a final stop at the West Valley Animal Shelter in Van Nuys. That's where they saw him for the first time. The Cockapoo—a designer cross between Cocker Spaniel and Poodle—had arrived at the shelter the day before. He had been wandering the streets of Mission Hills when someone turned him in. He was not neutered or microchipped. His overgrown, wavy, dingy locks were snarled and served as a canopy shielding his eyes.

Alaina and Matthew saw past the shabby coat. With melting hearts, they let the cutie sniff and lick their fingers through the spaces of the cage. Smiles on all three faces grew wider with each passing moment.

The couple wanted to take him out of his kennel to see how he interacted with them. Unfortunately, the Cockapoo wasn't allowed to come out and play just yet. The shelter held dogs for four days to see if an owner would come and claim them. During this waiting period, animals were not allowed out of their kennels.

The bars separating the couple from the pup did not stop a bond from forming. The friendly Cockapoo was clearly grateful for this delightful pair's visit. All Alaina and Matthew wanted to do was pet and play with their new friend. He was perfect! Perfectly adorable. Perfectly affectionate. Perfectly friendly.

The precious Cockapoo's four-day hold was up on Friday. Not only could he be let out of his cage to play, but he could also be adopted. Alaina and Matthew invited Alaina's mom to come meet their hopeful new family member. The three arrived at the shelter before it opened at 8:00 A.M. that day.

Alaina and Matthew's stomachs were spinning with excitement and a twinge of worry. If other people wanted this boy, then a silent auction would be held. All parties would write down an amount that they were willing to pay, and the highest bid would get to take home the Cockapoo. Who wouldn't want him? He was an incredible dog.

As they walked through the entry of the shelter, a new set of nerves swept over Alaina. "What if he's not the dog we think he is? I don't want to have to bring him back!"

"I'm confident your instincts are spot on. No need to worry about that, honey." Alaina's mom tried to ease her nerves.

Matthew was enthused, "Come on. Let's go meet him again!"

The three spent face-to-face time with the Cockapoo that morning. He was just as sweet outside his cage as he was through its bars. Alaina held the dog like a baby. When many dogs might squirm or wriggle in panic, this guy was chill—convincing Alaina that he was a pretty darn friendly dog. The couple were hooked. They wanted this dog! Fortunately, Alaina and Matthew did not have any competition. He was theirs. They were his.

First things first, the shelter required the Cockapoo be neutered and microchipped before taking him home. He also got his ragamuffin coat shaved. When Alaina and Matthew returned later that day to pick him up and bring him home, their brows crinkled with confusion when the technician brought him out. "Are you sure this is the right dog?" Matthew asked.

The technician checked the chart, looked at the dog, and confirmed with a smile, "Yes. He was neutered today. And, we also shaved his matted coat. This is your dog. Congratulations!"

"Oh, my gosh. He's bald! He looks like a totally different dog," Alaina laughed.

"It'll grow back, right buddy?" Matthew smiled and scratched their new dog behind the ears.

It didn't take long for Alaina and Matthew to fall in love with this guy. After having him home for an hour, Alaina declared, "He is the best thing ever!"

Now, he just needed a name. They deliberated and contemplated, then deliberated some more. With a mile-long list of names, it changed every day—some days every hour. He was "Bernie" for a day, but, like all the other names, it didn't seem to stick.

Nearly a week later, Matthew took the Cockapoo for his first official veterinarian check up. At this point, a decision needed to be made. As Matthew stood at the reception desk to check in, the receptionist asked, "What's your dog's name?"

There was a short pause. Remembering one of Alaina's favorite names from their list, Matthew blurted, "Elvis." He smiled, "Yeah, Elvis!"

Matthew explained a concern to the veterinarian, "This little dude's rib sticks out. He can lift one of his legs when he pees, but never the other."

Elvis

"Which one can't he lift?"

"The back left leg."

After examining Elvis, the vet explained, "He definitely broke a rib in the past. Only time will heal it, but he should be okay."

If only dogs could talk. Alaina and Matthew could only speculate about what may have happened. Perhaps he was beaten in his previous home? Maybe he was kicked by a stranger while living on the streets? No matter what might have happened, Elvis was now safe and already very much loved.

The vet was right. With time, the injury healed on its own. One evening when the three were out walking, Alaina's eyes suddenly grew wide with excitement. She squealed softly as she pointed at Elvis, "Look Matthew! Look!" He was lifting his left leg as he peed.

"That's awesome! His rib must be all healed up." They both kneeled down to give their sweet boy love and pets and kisses.

Alaina called her mom to share the good news. While chatting, Alaina's mom mentioned to her, "I'm not sure if you realize this, but the day you adopted Elvis is the same day that we adopted TC 21 years ago."

TC was short for "Too Cute" and was Alaina's childhood dog. She was a beautiful, extremely hyperactive Sheppard-Whippet mix, who lived a happy 14 years.

"Oh, wow! Really, Mom? That's pretty cool. It must be sign. Elvis was meant to be ours!"

It did take Elvis some time to decompress and come out of his shell, which is common with many dogs traumatized by living on the streets and in a high-stress shelter environment. For the first month in his new home, Elvis was extremely quiet. Even though he was showered with toys, he didn't play with them. Alaina mentioned her concern to Matthew. "I think Elvis might be boring!"

Elvis soon laid Alaina's concerns to rest. His personality bloomed like a happy spring flower and he proved himself to be an exemplary canine. In fact, Alaina and Matthew were stunned by how quickly he learned tricks. The little smarty could have joined the circus with his impressive repertoire—everything from high-fives to crawling on his belly like a soldier to strutting along in the pattern of an "8" between people's legs.

Elvis with Alaina

Elvis is a happy dog with a happy life. While visiting with friends, Alaina stroked her sweet pup. She said, "Elvis is never going to die, but, if he does, I will adopt again. It makes me feel so good that we went to the shelter to find Elvis. If we hadn't, he may have never been rescued."

3

CHANGING A HEART IS PAWSIBLE

Most kids like to go to the zoo to see animals. Julia and Becca's warm, compassionate hearts drew them to the local animal shelter instead. They went on a weekly basis to play with the cats and keep the dogs company. The sisters knew the P.D. Pitchford Companion Animal Village in Long Beach well because they both participated in the spcaLA Friends for Life Camp™ where they learned how to take care of pets and respect animals. They also learned basic dog training skills. Julia attended the camp for four summers and Becca went for three summers.

During the school year on walks home from school, Julia's friends would ask, "What do you guys want to do?"

Julia's eyes lit up, "How about we go to the animal shelter? I like to look at the dogs."

Her friends laughed, "That's weird! But, okay, let's go!"

For every birthday and Christmas, the girls begged their mom and dad to let them adopt a dog of their own.

"Please, Mom!" Julia pleaded. "All I want is a dog. I will take such good care of it!"

"No, Julia. I grew up with dogs. They are not just cute toys to play with and put away when you get bored. They are a lot of work. Feeding, water, walking, picking up poop. And, I know—I just know—I'm going to be the one who ends up having to do all the work. Besides, your dad and Becca are allergic."

Over the years, Julia and Becca continued to ask, while Michelle and Peter, their mom and dad, continued to resist. The sisters were practically obsessed. They both had dog dictionaries and memorized all the breeds by age five. Becca would read her thick dog dictionary for hours. Julia had a pocket sized one. She used it so much that the spine broke and pages were falling out.

On walks or car rides, instead of playing "slug bug," they would spot and identify dogs.

"Hey, Julia. There's a Shih Tzu!"

"Oh! How cute is she?"

Michelle's mom always had dogs, so the girls were able to get their dog fix partially satisfied when they spent one day a week at their grandmother's house. They told friends and new acquaintances all about their dog, claiming their grandma's dog as their own. When those friends came over to their house to hang out, they inevitably asked to meet their dog. With silly grins, the girls explained, "Well, he doesn't live here, but we really do have a dog!"

When Julia was 15 and Becca was 10, the girls went on another weekly adventure to the animal shelter with their grandma. They met a little white dog named Peaches.

"Julia, let's call Mom. Maybe we can get her to come down here. He is so cute! Isn't he, Grandma?"

"Oh, he is adorable. He might just be hypoallergenic, too."

"Okay, I'll try! Be right back."

Julia returned. "Oh, my gosh. She must be in a really good mood. She's on her way."

"Yes!" Becca excitedly hugged her grandma.

As soon as Michelle arrived, she started throwing out stern objections. "I'm only here to see the dog. We can't have a dog. I don't want a dog."

"Okay, okay, Mom. But, just come on." Julia led her to the bonding room and Becca and Grandma followed.

The shelter worker brought the little white dog to meet them.

"He is so hyper!" Julia laughed.

"Is he ever," Becca agreed with her sister.

Michelle just shook her head in disbelief and asked herself, "What am I doing here?"

In hopes of finding the perfect dog for this family, the shelter worker thought about a good match and one particular cutie came to mind. "There's another adorable little dog you might like. He's a Poodle and possibly Jack Russell mix. He's hypoallergenic, too. Wait right here. I will bring him to you."

Moments later, Oliver walked into the room.

"He is perfect." Julia couldn't stop smiling.

"Oh, my gosh. Mom! Isn't he the cutest? He's a little monster!" Becca's eyes twinkled with happiness.

With a completely unexplainable shift in thinking, Michelle made a suggestion to her girls. "Let's bring Dad tomorrow to meet him." She turned to the shelter worker, "Can we put him on hold?"

The shelter worker smiled and nodded, "Yes, of course."

Julia and Becca were jumping in their seats with excitement, while their grandmother looked on with a delighted grin.

The family went back the next day—this time with Dad in tow—and played with the "little monster" in the bonding room. Peter grew up with cats. He was indifferent to dogs, but this one made him smile.

After giving the family some time alone with the dog, the shelter worker returned to take him back to his cage. While she slipped the leash on, Michelle asked, "This is a no-kill shelter, right?"

The woman replied, "No. Unfortunately, it's not. We only have so much space."

Michelle was silent and thought to herself, "Oh, boy. I'm getting roped in."

The shelter worker headed toward the door with the leashed dog. The little guy stopped in his tracks and planted his feet firmly to the ground. He wasn't going anywhere. He liked this family! The shelter worker had to pick him up and carry him away.

Michelle was the first to speak after the door closed. "That's it. He's ours."

Julia looked at her mom with a mix of elation and shock. "Really, Mom? Do you mean it?"

Suddenly, Michelle realized what she was committing to. "If we're going to get this dog, there are going to be rules. He's small, so he will be in the house. No getting on the sofa. No climbing on the beds. He strictly needs to be on the floor. Each one of us walks him once a day. Got it?"

"Got it!" The girls chimed together in pure glee.

After spending who-knows-how-long wandering and surviving on city streets, followed by seven days in an intimidating animal shelter, Oliver was welcomed with loving arms into a warm, caring home.

He was a mess. His matted fur was greasy, dirty, and flea-infested. It camouflaged the outline of his rib cage on a fragile, underweight body. Oliver's paws were wrapped in bandages because they were worn and torn from pounding the pavement for so long. To top it off, his neck was adorned with the cone of shame after being neutered. In tough shape and scared, he sat timidly in a corner of his new home for hours.

It took Oliver a while to come out of his shell, but his family was patient. They put themselves in his shoes—or in his case, bandaged paws—to understand his fears. For a year, Oliver refused to leave the front yard to go for a walk. Michelle would pick him up, carry him for two blocks, and then put him down. With intense focus, he hurriedly led Michelle straight back home. It was his safe haven.

Oliver with Julia (left) and Becca (right)

Oliver was afraid of everything. He was afraid of people. Heck, he was even afraid of the wind. He was especially afraid of his leash if it was loose and dangling. He preferred it to be taut. If one of Oliver's humans got tangled in the leash and lifted their foot to escape, Oliver cowered back in fear. If his retractable leash fell and the handle banged against the floor, he would panic and freak out.

His new family loved him anyway. They all rallied around Oliver. The biggest surprise was how much Michelle came to adore him. More than once, Peter arrived home and was sure someone was visiting when he heard Michelle having a full-on conversation about her day. As he rounded the corner, he saw it was just her and Oliver. "Hey, honey. Who are you talking to?"

"Oliver! He knows what I'm saying. Plus, he never sasses back to me."

Peter shook his head and smiled as he leaned over to give his wife a peck on the cheek. Then, he walked over to Oliver to scratch his head, "Hey, little guy!"

For Oliver's first Christmas with the family, there was a present labeled, "To our family; From our family." Michelle was overflowing with excitement and kept telling the girls, "There's a really special present for all of us! You're going to love it. It's for all of us!"

Finally, Christmas arrived. It cannot be said who was more excited about the gift—the person who gave it, Michelle—or, those who received it, Peter, Julia, and Becca. They opened the highly-anticipated package together. As if on cue, three sets of eyes popped and three jaws dropped. Soon after, laughter ensued. It was a giant printed replica of Andy Warhol's famous *Marilyn Diptych* pop art painting with the same photograph replicated in four different colored squares: blue, pink, yellow, green. Instead of a photograph of Marilyn Monroe, it was a photograph of Oliver.

"Aren't you so excited? Isn't this the best Christmas ever?" Michelle was beaming.

To this day, the giant picture sits on the ledge over the fireplace in the family room. It is accompanied by two small pictures—one of each of the girls. Clearly, Oliver is king of the household.

Oliver

Over the span of a couple of years, Oliver morphed from a frightened, timid pup to a playful, quirky little guy with a huge personality. He loves to play fetch in the house. To get attention, he brings a ball into either Julia or Becca's room, pushes it under the nightstand with his nose, and then playfully growls at it until someone comes to get it out for him.

When Oliver is thirsty, but too tired to go downstairs to the water bowl, he sits in the bathtub and waits for someone to come turn on the water. If he waits too long, he sends a request to his family with his talking-voice rumble, which gets louder and louder the longer he has to wait.

At bedtime, Oliver is like a toddler that doesn't want to miss out on anything. As soon as he hears, "Oliver, it's bedtime!" he puts up a little fuss. Michelle calls it "civil disobedience" because his body gets so stiff that nobody can pick him up to tuck him in to his crate.

When morning comes, Oliver is raring to go. Michelle tells him, "Go wake up Rebecca!" He runs to her door and jumps on her bed as Michelle follows. It always turns into a two-person pet time for Oliver, getting morning love and rubs from both Rebecca and Michelle.

Oliver with his forever family (clockwise from top left):
Michelle, Peter, Becca and Julia

Oliver unifies the entire family. Julia thinks he makes them all nicer people. On a personal level, he inspires her. So much so that she created a video about dog rescue that got her into her dream college. When Julia had her high school senior photo taken, she brought Oliver. One of the family's favorite photos is of Julia in her cap and gown with Oliver wearing a little graduation cap of his own.

Oliver also inspired Julia to volunteer three times a week for a summer at Bichons and Buddies rescue out of Culver City, California. Her hope is that others will find dogs that they love as much as she and her family love Oliver. They can't imagine life without him.

4

ADOPTING A SENIOR DOG IS PAWSIBLE

Lyndsay and Jenn both grew up in Pasadena, California, and have been best friends since high school. After graduation, Jenn went off to Boston University. During her last year, Lyndsay decided to join her dear pal and experience all that the great historic city had to offer. They would often venture out into the neighborhood and inevitably spot people walking their adorable dogs. "Oh my gosh, Jenn. Look at that cutie! What breed is that?"

"Hmmm. Maybe some sort of Shepherd mix? So beautiful! We should really adopt a dog. How great would that be?"

The conversation of adopting a dog came up often. After Jenn finished school in Boston, the two young women returned to Pasadena and decided to go visit the dogs at the local Humane Society. They were open to the possibility of bringing home a dog, but it was not their intention.

As they walked through the kennels, they spotted a white, curly-haired dog that was trying to hide in the back of her cage. The two friends continued walking along until they reached the end of the kennel row. When they turned around to come back, they both saw it at the same time, looked at each other and said, "Aw!" As they peered down the rows of kennels, a white paw was sticking out, reaching for them through the bars.

Approaching the sweet pup's kennel, they knelt down to let her lick their hands through the bars as she continued to reach out her paw to them. She was the only dog in the kennel that wasn't barking. Instead, her human-like eyes were fixated on Lyndsay and Jenn.

"Jenn, she's telling us to save her. Look at those eyes!"

"They are so soulful."

Since moving back to Pasadena, the young women both lived with their parents, who were neighbors. Lyndsay considered living options for this sweetie out loud, "My parents would be totally cool with having a dog stay at their house. It could be her home base. You are family, so you could come and spend time with her whenever you want. What do you think? I just don't think I can take care of her on my own, but if we adopt her together ... well, that's completely doable."

As they continued discussing their care strategies to give this girl the best life possible, they overheard a couple inquiring about the dog to people who worked at the shelter. Jenn and Lyndsay looked at each other with big eyes. They both knew they needed to act fast to take this girl home.

"Let's do it!" Jenn was filled with excitement.

Before they could bring her home, Pasadena Humane Society & SPCA (PSH) required that the dog meets everyone in the household to ensure a congenial and successful adoption. As Lyndsay, her parents, and Jenn sat in a visiting room at PSH, the canine entered and traipsed around the room, happily greeting one person after another. She knew what she was doing. She wanted to go home with this family, and her wish came true: The adoption was approved!

The cream-colored Goldendoodle with an ultra matted coat was the epitome of an "unadoptable dog." Her teeth were shattered, probably from living on the streets and eating trash. In fact, she didn't even have any front teeth. Since her fur was so painfully matted, Lyndsay and Jenn had her shaved at the shelter—all the way to the skin—before bringing her home. That's when an army of tumors was discovered. They had invaded her entire body and, to this point, had been camouflaged by her snarled curls. This girl needed lots of love and care. Lyndsay and Jenn were ready to surround her with an abundance of both.

Although Lyndsay's parents welcomed their daughter's new canine friend into their home with open arms, the shaved canine displayed great reserve with them and stuck to Lyndsay and Jenn's sides like glue. Lyndsay's mom took no offense. She suggested the old dog needed a new name.

"Why don't you call her Lucy?"

Lyndsay and Jenn hemmed and hawed about it for a little while, but soon agreed it was a perfect fit. One of their favorite shows was the classic, "I Love Lucy."

On Lucy's first evening in her new home, a horrible seizure overtook her. Lyndsay and Jenn watched helplessly as she convulsed, foamed at the mouth, and lost control of her bladder. When the event ceased, she was dazed and walked around the house aimlessly. It took about 30 minutes for her to return to her normal self.

The girls had no idea what to do. After taking Lucy to see the vet, they discovered a few important facts about her health. Based on her teeth, the vet put her age at about 13 or 14 years old, and delivered good news about all the tumors that had taken over her body. They were noncancerous.

"Whew!" Lyndsay and Jenn looked at each other with great relief.

The vet continued explaining and showed the girls, "Unfortunately, two are located here between her hip bones and causing Lucy a lot of pain when she sits down. I would recommend having them removed. Now, regarding the seizure she had last night, Lucy has epilepsy. The good news is that there is medication I can prescribe for her. If you give it to her two times a day, you should be able to keep the seizures under control."

With proper medical treatment and plenty of love and attention from Lyndsay and Jenn, Lucy magically morphed from a sickly stray to a gorgeous, healthy, happy doggy. Amazed by her physical transformation. Lyndsay and Jenn could not get enough of their sweet girl, and their sweet girl was growing quite enamored of them. The same could not be said about any other humans in Lucy's life.

Despite the gregarious initial meeting at PSH, Lucy continued being shy around Lyndsay's parents. She was apprehensive of all people except Lyndsay and Jenn. In fact, she was petrified of men. Lyndsay's dad would try bribe her affection with bacon, but she wouldn't go near him.

When Lyndsay and Jenn went on a vacation, Lucy went into her dog house and did not come out until they returned. Lyndsay's parents tried their best to gain her trust, but Lucy was fearful of everyone and everything. All Lyndsay's mom could do was put food and water inside Lucy's doghouse.

It was pretty clear to everyone that Lucy had been abused at some point in her life. Due to her medical problems, she made quite a few visits to the vet, oftentimes getting x-rays. Vets would ask, "Do you know anything about her past? Was she abused?"

"We really don't know anything. Is there something you see?"

"The x-rays show BB gun pellets."

"Maybe she ingested them?"

"No, there's a puncture wound here. She was shot at with a BB gun."

Hearing news like this made Lyndsay and Jenn love this sweet, quiet girl even more. They did everything in their power to make her life as happy as possible. By keeping up with her medication, Lucy's epilepsy remained under control. The seizures still happened, but not as frequently. Over the course of her first year with her new family, Lucy became more and more comfortable. She still kept her distance from anyone who wasn't Lyndsay or Jenn, but she got brave enough to leave their sides and run around like any happy dog does.

Two years after adopting Lucy, Lyndsay and Jenn were again admiring her transformation.

"Jenn, just look at Lucy. She is a gorgeous dog! Remember what she looked like the day we adopted her?"

"She was a mess! Do we have any pictures of her from that time?"

"Shoot. Ya know? I don't think so."

"Maybe we can go to the shelter and get one. Do you think they'd have it on file, Lyndsay?"

The pair headed back the Pasadena PSH. They had no intention of adopting another dog.

"Since we're here, Lyndsay, we might as well take a stroll around."

They did and history repeated itself. A furry white paw reached out to Jenn and Lyndsay between the bars. When they arrived to see who was reeling them in, a pleading, yet playful pair of eyes pulled them in even further. The dog's name was Paddington and he looked just like Lucy, but smaller.

This five year old Wheaton Terrier-Schnauzer mix was down on his luck. He had been adopted twice and returned twice. Lyndsay and Jenn agreed, they needed to save another dog. They also agreed, he needed a new name. It was a no-brainer.

"Welcome to the family, Desi!"

Desi

If ever there were two opposites, it was Desi and Lucy. They had two things in common: 1) They both adored Lyndsay and Jenn; 2) They were both fearful. Each handled their fear differently. Lucy ran to safety, while Desi confronted it head on. Physically, this spunky boy was healthy. However, he did have some aggression issues. He lunged at big trucks, skateboarders, postal carriers, the elderly, strollers, disabled people—essentially, anyone or anything that was out of the ordinary to him.

Despite his aggressive behavior, Desi was never aggressive toward Lucy. While Desi was very playful, youthful and energetic, Lucy was peaceful, quiet and slow. At times, Lucy licked Desi to groom him. He really valued his personal space, but let her do it. He was patient with her.

Lucy had no idea how big she was. From time to time, she would stomp on Desi in the middle of the night, but he would do nothing. They would sleep butt to butt—no cuddling, but always touching.

The duo balanced each other out. A very serene Lucy was energized by Desi's puppy-like behavior. When it came time to determine which noises to worry about and which ones to brush off, Desi followed Lucy's lead. Lucy infused a bit of calm into Desi. She never reacted when he barked.

As the years went by, Lucy was an old dog getting older. Tumors and cysts were constantly popping up. At the same time, her seizures were becoming more frequent. She would get seizures every other day for a week, and then a week would pass without any. The next week she'd have them again every other day, and then none the following week. This went on and on.

One of her tumors started growing quite large. Eventually, it reached the size of a football. Lyndsay and Jenn took her to the vet and had to ask themselves hard questions. Should we put her down? Is she suffering? It is moments like this when you wish your dog could speak. Lucy couldn't tell Lyndsay and Jenn whether she was in misery.

On one of their clinic visits, they turned to the vet for advice, "We are really scared to put her down. What should we do?"

"The decision is in your hands. You know Lucy best."

Lucy was still eating regularly. She was still trying to jump on the couch to sit with her favorite people. Her emotional state wasn't changing, but her physical health was a completely different story. It was taking a toll on her. The huge tumor made it difficult for Lucy to lay down, but she was too old for surgery to have it removed. Lyndsay and Jenn were in turmoil over the right thing to do and decided to take her to another vet to get a second opinion.

Lyndsay purposefully went to work early on the day of the second vet appointment—so she could return early and get Lucy there on time. Usually, Lucy got up with Lyndsay. On this particular morning, she chose to stay in bed. Not wanting to disturb her rest, Lyndsay bent down and whispered, "Goodbye, sweet Lucy." She gave her pets and kisses, while admiring her beloved girl. Lucy was breathing and blinked to acknowledge Lyndsay's goodbye.

A few moments later, Jenn stopped by to see Lucy. With her deteriorating health over the past month, Jenn made a habit of visiting Lucy in the mornings before work. She gave her loving, gentle pets and kissed Lucy goodbye. Lucy looked at Jenn with tired, admiring, soulful eyes.

Over her lunch break, Jenn returned. Desi greeted her at the front door in his usual happy, crazy state. "Hey, buddy! How are you? Let's go check on Lucy."

As Jenn entered Lindsay's room, a still coldness swept over her. Lucy was gone. Her lifeless body was still on Lyndsay's bed, but it was just that. Her body. Her soul—her sweet life—was gone.

As if auto-pilot kicked in, Jenn picked up Lucy's body and took her to the car. Oblivious to what happened, Desi excitedly jumped into the car. He was ready and raring to go on a ride to the park.

"No, Desi. Come on. Back inside. Good boy." Jenn pet his head, then closed the front door. In a trance-like state, she got into the driver's seat of her car and just sat there. "Is this really happening?"

She turned to look at Lucy in the back seat. After taking a deep breath, she called Lyndsay, "Hey. Lucy was really sick when I checked on her over lunch. I'm taking her to the animal hospital. Will you meet us there?"

"Oh, no. Yes! I'm leaving now."

Jenn couldn't tell Lyndsay just yet. She didn't want her driving in a state of high emotions. She wanted her best friend to arrive at the animal hospital safely.

To keep her own emotions under control as she drove, Jenn imagined that Lucy was only asleep in the back seat. It was a 30 minute drive. She had to do her best to detach herself from her heartbreaking loss.

Jenn arrived at the animal hospital with Lucy before Lyndsay. The kind staff provided them with a private room. When Lyndsay got there, Jenn explained what happened.

Both young women gave Lucy a hug, held her for a short while, and said goodbye.

"Oh, Jenn. This is rough. My heart hurts so much. Let's go somewhere. Let's get a drink."

The best friends spent the rest of the afternoon reminiscing about their sweet girl who had lived such a hard life.

"I am so grateful that we were able to give her the good life she deserved these past five years, Lyndsay."

"She was in such rough shape when we adopted her. I can't believe she survived so long."

With a thoughtful glimmer in her eye, Jenn said, "Maybe she hung onto life for so long for us."

Jenn smiled through her tears. "She deserved all the love we gave her. She was a such a sweet, sweet girl. I already miss her so much."

"Me, too."

The two headed back to Lyndsay's home to see Desi. He greeted both women with a big dose of happy as they walked through the door.

"Hi, boy!" Lyndsay smiled and knelt down to give him pets as he licked her face.

"Desi!" Jenn joined in the joy fest as the silly dog smothered her in kisses, too.

After he calmed down a little, Jenn smiled at him, admiring his eyes. "Desi has such playful puppy eyes. So different from Lucy. There was something about her eyes. She could just look at you, and it was so piercing. She had something special. She was an old soul. Dogs definitely have souls."

Lyndsay reached out to her friend and gave her a teary-eyed hug.

Desi with Jenn (left) and Lyndsay (right) admiring a photo of Lucy

To this day, Desi is an energetic trickster who can't get enough of running and playing. Even though he has his own bed, he sneaks into Lyndsay's bed every night to be near her while she sleeps. On week days, the lucky boy gets to go to work with Lyndsay. When the weekend comes, he loves camping or visiting the ocean. He is not averse to barking and running after the waves. Desi is a happy, much-loved boy.

5

INTERCONNECTEDNESS IS PAWSIBLE

In late summer 2003, life was looking great. I was settled in my new condo, Filbert and Monroe were happy, and I started dating a kind, funny, dog-loving guy named Jason.

Monroe started scooting. He did this every nine months or so. It's that thing some dogs do when they need their anal glands expressed. In a seated position with their butthole glued to the carpet and their hind legs slightly elevated in front of them, they use their front legs to scoot along the floor like a windup toy. Too afraid I would either hurt him or squirt myself in the eye with foul-smelling pheromone secretions, I chose to take him to the vet to get his anal glands expressed.

I noticed he was needing this done more frequently than normal. I also noticed he was having trouble pooping. Over the course of a few months, I took him to my veterinarian three different times. The vet claimed nothing was wrong with him.

I disagreed and mentioned my concerns to Jason. With high praise, he referred me to his trusted veterinarian. "She's amazing!"

Monroe endured brief poking and prodding in a not-so-fun area. Within just a few minutes of examining him, the vet took off her gloves and turned to me.

Kindly, she explained, "You were right to get a second opinion. I am concerned about a lump. I have an excellent oncologist that I'm going to refer you to. I suggest you make the appointment as soon as possible."

"What do you think is wrong?"

"A tumor in the prostate is rare, but extremely serious. I cannot be sure of what I am feeling. The oncologist will run tests and be able to give you a definitive prognosis. The oncology center I'm referring you to is excellent. They will walk you through everything."

I was stunned. Nervous butterflies fluttered quickly with worry in my stomach. Monroe was only 7 years old. I was certain that his life was only half over.

"Cancer?" My eyes welled with tears.

"It's very possible. I'm so sorry. But, like I said, the oncologist will be able to figure out exactly what is wrong."

A week later, in early December, the oncologist performed an ultrasound on Monroe, took thoracic radiographs, and ran some other tests.

"Ms. Kurtz, I have some tough news to share. There is a cancerous tumor in Monroe's prostate. Prostate tumors are typically aggressive and highly invasive. It's hard to say at this point exactly how aggressive."

"What can we do?" I was focused on fixing Monroe.

"We can do chemotherapy and radiation therapy. He would undergo one chemotherapy treatment, which would be succeeded by seven radiation treatments. The side effects are minimal in dogs. The procedure is not nearly as intense or invasive as it is on humans. In the end, the result would be a reduced tumor size, and, hopefully, the elimination of cancer cells spreading throughout his body."

"How much time would he have?"

"It depends how effective the treatment is. It could be as few as two months. Maybe six months. If the treatment is highly effective, as long as a year."

Initially, I struggled to make a decision. I didn't want to give in to cancer or give up hope. Many people thought otherwise, including Jason. I knew Monroe would do anything for me. I had to do all in my power for him.

Determination combined with a fair amount of denial led to my firm decision to fight for Monroe. After my mind was made up, Jason was incredibly supportive. Dog sitting. Coming with me to oncology appointments. Just being there.

Monroe responded well to his six week treatment plan. In the process, he quickly became a staff favorite, and made many new highly compassionate human friends.

His life became a wondrous world of new adventures intertwined with old routines. We took a road trip into the mountains to once again romp through the snow. We went on numerous explorations through the woods. We enjoyed countless cuddles. He even learned how to use a doggy door.

Monroe's handholding sessions on the couch became more frequent. He used his nose to persistently nudge my arm until I held out my hand to hold his paw.

Together, we were introduced to a desert ranch where Monroe ran fast and free. He raced across the open space with effortless grace grinning from ear to ear. It was glorious to watch. Exhilarating. Invigorating.

As an amateur photographer, Jason captured many of these incredible memories beautifully. Three months after Monroe started treatment, Jason was dog sitting and took him to the park. They had their own private photo shoot.

Later that day after work, I stopped by Jason's house to pick up both Monroe and Filbert.

"Tes, I need to show you something. I took some photos of Monroe today."

His reddish brown fur with white markings on his face, chest, and feet were in stunning contrast to the lush background of green bushes and grass. Monroe was sitting perfectly poised. His presence was strong, yet his body was frail. His focused eyes pierced the camera lens. They spoke, "I'm done."

"Monroe has been hanging on for you, Tes. It's time to let him go."

I knew it was true. My balloon of denial burst in that moment.

With little appetite, Roe had been losing weight over the last couple of weeks. He no longer smelled like his doggy self. Instead, he emitted a strange, cancerous odor.

Jason was right. It was time.

On the morning of Monroe's final day on earth, Jason and I took him to his favorite park. We treated him to a McDonald's hamburger as he delighted in the spring breeze delivered by a beautiful March day.

Later, the three of us arrived at the oncologist's office and were taken to a private room. Monroe laid relaxed on a wide bench that was affixed to the wall. Jason sat next to him near his head. I sat on the floor in front of him admiring my gorgeous, sweet boy. This boy who brought so much joy, support, adventure, and love into my life.

"I will give you some time to say goodbye." Roe's oncologist was an extraordinary woman. She and her staff showed immense compassion for Monroe and I every step of this arduous, yet cherished and precious journey.

After she exited the room, I caressed Monroe's thin, weak body. "Thank you for loving me, Monroe. I know you love me so much. I am the reason you hung on so tight. Now, it's my turn to give you the gift of peace."

Jason said his sweet goodbye. We both poured all our love over Monroe.

Monroe's oncologist quietly returned and gently asked, "Are you ready?"

Through tears, I softly, nearly inaudibly, answered, "Yes."

As I continued to kneel before Monroe, I lovingly held his face in my hands as he was put to a peaceful, forever sleep.

Slowly, I felt him drift away. His soul lifted. It consumed me for a brief moment. Then, suddenly, the room was unbearably cold. His body was there, but the essence of Roe was gone. The cold suffocated me. I had to leave. Immediately.

I darted out of the room and the building. As I stepped outside, a crisp gust of spring fanned my tearful face. I felt him. Roe's spirit was in the air. I breathed him in. The breeze continued to sprinkled me with his being.

Jason ran out seconds after me. We stood side by side with the Monroe-filled breeze sweeping through us. Every part of nature jumped out at us. The trees. The clouds. The flowers. Everything was vivid. Everything was fresh. Everything was new. Monroe's soul enveloped my surroundings.

"Oh, my gosh. Do you feel that, Tes?" Jason, too, was overcome by Monroe's spirit.

I smiled through a never-ending stream of tears. "He's everywhere. Monroe is everywhere!"

Shortly after Monroe passed, Jason and I parted ways. Those few months we shared with Monroe were a precious, beautifully wrapped gift that I placed in my heart for safekeeping.

So, it was just Filbert and me. My Happy Papi loved having me all to himself, which he did for several months. By the time summer rolled around, I started yearning for another dog to save.

I wasn't sure if I was ready, but something—some being—was calling me.

I checked online for Basenji mixes. Filbert and I met a couple of wonderful dogs available for adoption through rescue organizations that were not quite a good match for either my schedule or Filbert's personality. Then, one day in mid-August, I spotted a handsome boy on the website listings for Noah's Bark Rescue based in Manhattan Beach, California. Listed as a Shepherd mix, his name was Chance.

I felt a strong pull toward him. It was in the eyes. The windows to this boy's deep soul were so similar to Monroe's. Thick black liner outlined his almond-shaped, chocolaty-browns.

Even though he was listed on the rescue's website, he was currently being treated for illness in the good care of a foster. I decided to apply to adopt him, anyway. I had faith he would be fine. On the application, I wrote:

"I understand that Chance is not quite ready for adoption. Whenever he is, I am ready to open my heart and home to him. Thank you for your consideration."

Within 24 hours, my application was approved. His foster mom, Gerrie, reached out to me via email to tell me that he was lethargic and not eating well. He was being treated for tapeworm, roundworm, and kennel cough. She would keep me posted on his health.

My heart sank.

Two weeks later, my heart lifted. Gerrie told me that even though he still had a cough, he was eating well and his energy was up. In fact, he was quite rambunctious. She invited me to meet him. I did, and I fell in love.

Despite his cough, he was a high-energy goofball. He had a smile that lit up the room and filled my heart with happiness. I met him in the presence of five or six other foster dogs. They were hard to count. I couldn't figure out how Gerrie did it. I was in awe of her ability to take in and care for so many dogs. A true hero, in my book.

Even with all the other canines and people surrounding us, Chance and I just clicked. He was the one.

Curious about his history, I asked Gerrie, "How did he end up with Noah's Bark and in your care?"

"As you can tell, I foster a lot of dogs. I'm always fostering! My daughter found him running the streets of Torrance in the rain. I couldn't take him in at the time and she was going out of town. She took him to Carson shelter. She thought she would be back in less than a week to get him out, and we'd figure out a foster. Her return was delayed. His time was up at the shelter. It's so overcrowded, the dogs usually only get a week or so. Well, the guy working there thought he was such a cool dog, he decided to give him another week, a second chance. He's also the one who named him Chance. A couple days later, my daughter, Brittany, returned to LA, and was able to get him out of the shelter. Space opened up here, too."

I listened in near disbelief at all this dog had been through during his first year of life. Gerrie kept me updated during the following weeks. The cough lingered. In late September, there was a change:

"Tes, I'm sorry to tell you that Chance has taken a turn for the worse. The veterinarian who has been treating him highly suspects that he has distemper. We haven't run the test to confirm it because it is an expensive test to run, and we'd rather use the funds toward getting him better. I will update you as soon as I can. Right now, it's touch and go."

There is no cure to destroy the distemper virus. Fifty percent of adult dogs that get it survive. Only twenty percent of puppies survive it. Chance was in my thoughts constantly. I prayed for him every day.

On the first weekend in October, I went to visit my brother and his family in Bakersfield. I couldn't sleep. When this happens, I often step outside to look at the stars. I did exactly that.

The night was cool. The clear, dark sky was decorated with endless sparkling stars. With Chance on my mind, I took a deep breath in, closed my eyes, and tilted my head skyward. With great faith I asked, "Please, dear God. Please give Chance the strength to pull through this. Please help him get healthy."

I exhaled and opened my eyes. The beautiful night sky delivered a shooting star. It took my breath away. My hope was replaced with faith—faith that Chance would be okay.

Two days later, I received a note from Gerrie:

"I have great news! Miraculously, Chance is fully recovered. You can come pick him up anytime!"

Four days later, Filbert and I went to pick him up. When I knocked on Gerrie's door, Chance was right there to greet me. He remembered me!

To say the transition of Chance becoming part of our family was smooth, well, it would be a complete lie. It was a disaster.

He ate numerous pairs of both designer and not-so-designer shoes, a CD, his plastic food bowl, one-and-a-half TV remotes, and my two-year-old nephew's Sponge Bob Square Pants birthday piñata. The final straw came when he decided to rip up my carpet.

I decided that I was going to get hardwood floors anyway. I forgave him.

Then, he threw me over the edge. On a walk through my condominium complex, Chance nipped my priest on his lower calf. The kind, old, small Irishman was also my neighbor. He lifted up his pant leg to show me the scratch mark left by Chance's tooth, and asked, "Will I get rabies?"

"Oh, no. No, he's up to date on shots. You won't get rabies. Are you okay? I'm so sorry."

I was done.

I couldn't take any more.

I was sending him back.

But, I couldn't.

I couldn't give up on him.

I didn't give up on him.

Instead, I loved him and became the pack leader he needed.

I didn't realize the breed of dog I had on my hands. I learned he was an Australian Kelpie. A highly intelligent and highly energetic working dog. This dog needed training and a job.

We bonded during group dog training classes and practices. We also became running partners. I taught him how to catch fly balls and fetch ground balls. He became an awesome Frisbee dog. We soon became regulars at the dog park where Chance found a balance between play and work.

As much as he loved to catch his Frisbee, the more dogs that showed up at the park, the more apt he was to work.

Once in a while, he would find a dog his own size to wrestle and run with. More often than not, he liked to patrol the outer edge making sure everyone was in their proper place and getting along. Chance was especially enamored by smaller dogs and was quick to come to their rescue if ever their space became invaded by another dog. This was especially true of Filbert. Chance adored Filbert, and after his initial annoyance of no longer being a single dog, Filbert grew to love Chance. He looked to him for protection and friendship.

Even after training and getting him on an active lifestyle regime, Chance remained mischievous. He was a habitual counter surfer. Leaving him alone with something on the counter was a big no-no.

My mom and stepdad stayed with me over Christmas three years after I adopted Chance. My mom worked for a school and received mounds of gifts from students. Many of the gifts were festive holiday foods. Knowing she and her husband would never be able to eat all of the Christmas treats alone, she brought them to my place so we could all indulge.

We stacked several wrapped gifts on the kitchen counter and pushed them back against the wall. I turned on the TV for Filbert and Chance for background noise, as I always did when I left them alone. Off we went to a movie.

Two hours later, we returned to an extraordinary sight. My brain took a vibrant snapshot and the image will never leave my memory.

A delicately unwrapped two-pound box of See's chocolate candies was sitting on the living room floor in front of the TV. The holiday wrapping paper was thoughtfully cast aside, along with the lid to the chocolate candy box. Each individual brown wrapper was neatly piled to the right of the bottom of the empty See's box. The wrappers were aligned in such a way that it looked as if the culprit had intentionally planted himself in front of the TV and savored each chocolate candy one by one as he caught his favorite television show.

Two pounds of chocolate and nuts were devoured. Not one single morsel was left behind.

Initially, I was perplexed. Was this the doing of a human? Who broke into my house to binge on one box of chocolates in front of the TV?

That thought was fleeting. This chocolate party had Chance written all over it. Filbert never got into anything. Well, maybe my dirty underwear, which would magically appear in the living room at inappropriate times. But, that was it. He was finicky.

After solving the "whodunit" mystery, my heart sank. All of the evidence in this plot was a toxic nightmare for dogs.

I quickly Googled chocolate and dogs. The ratio of Chance's weight to the amount of chocolate he gorged himself with was borderline lethal. I took him to the emergency animal hospital where they induced vomiting, and then gave him activated charcoal mixed with water by mouth to flush out all of the toxins.

"For tonight, you might want to keep him in the garage or somewhere else that's closed off, but safe. He may have trouble controlling his bowels."

They weren't kidding. I tried to keep him inside, but he was antsy and had to go to the bathroom every few minutes. I put him in the garage to spend the night. I felt awful for him.

The next morning, the garage floors, walls, and everything in it were covered with black liquid charcoal. Not fun to clean, but man, oh man was I grateful he was okay.

Despite his grand shenanigans, Chance and I had a strong bond that only continued to get stronger over time. We have our own private mutual admiration society.

His incredibly strong will to live is inspiring, and his exuberance for the small things in life—feeling an ocean breeze, catching a ball or Frisbee, eating food, going for a run or walk—is greater than any I have ever witnessed. He is grateful for life's gifts. He is grateful for me. My heart overflows with gratitude for him.

6

OPENING YOUR HEART TO LOVE AGAIN IS PAWSIBLE

Dave and his Staffordshire Terrier mix, Sunny, did everything together. They ran, hiked, biked. Anything Dave did, Sunny did. It had been this way since she was a wee puppy.

Time has a way of sneaking up on us. Suddenly, Sunny was 15 years old. She could no longer do all the fun activities she loved to do with her human, Dave. He took his girl to the vet.

"What should I do?"

"It's not my place to advise, Dave. The decision is yours, but I think you will know in your heart when the time is right to let her go."

Dave hung his head and looked into Sunny's eyes as tears welled up in his own.

In her own way, Sunny let Dave know when she was ready. It was a heart-crushing goodbye.

A few years passed. Dave carried the memory of Sunny close to his heart. He was hesitant to even think about getting another dog.

One morning, Dave's fiancé, Katie, and his daughter, Rachel, were chatting over breakfast. Katie walked out to the living room to find her soon-to-be husband.

"Honey, Rachel and I were thinking about going to Pet Network to see the dogs up for adoption. What do you think? Join us?"

"I don't think so, Sweetie. I'm just not sure if we should get a dog at this point. I mean, it's a big commitment. Plus, I don't know whether I'm ready for a new dog."

"Oh, Dave." Katie gave her fiancé a warm hug and looked up at him with big, hopeful eyes. "Sunny was so loved. If there's a dog out there that you could love even half that much…well, he would be an extremely fortunate dog. What do you say?"

"Dad, pleeeaase! Please come with us to look at the puppies at the rescue."

"Oh, my gosh. You two have been sweet talking me for months about this. I can't resist anymore! I will go, but only for about half an hour. I have a bike ride this afternoon."

Off the trio went to Pet Network Humane Society in Incline, Nevada, near Lake Tahoe. Katie went straight to a litter of tiny and precious six-week-old puppies, while another cute young one caught Rachel's attention.

"Rachel, you have to come see these tiny babies. They are so adorable!"

Rachel walked over to check out the puppy litter. "Aw. They are super cute!" As adorable as they were, someone else had already won over Rachel's affections. After some coochy-coos with the puppies, she was drawn back to play with an adorable three-month-old Black Lab.

"Where are you going, Rach?"

"You gotta come here! Come meet this sweet Black Lab." She motioned for both of them to follow her.

"Okay, coming." Before she went to check out the Lab, she had to melt her husband's heart. "Dave, aren't these the cutest puppies you've ever seen? I would love to bring one of these little guys home!"

"They are pretty cute!" Although he said it and meant it, he kept a safe distance.

"Guys! Come here!" Rachel was determined that her parents meet the young pup with whom it took her merely seconds to fall in love.

"Rachel, he adores you." Katie's eyes lit up as she watched Rachel play with this young canine. He had a disposition as sweet as milk chocolate.

"Can we bring him home?"

Katie was ready to say, "Yes! Let's do it. Let's adopt him!" She held her tongue as she watched Dave.

Dave wasn't about to fall for this boy so easily. With his guard up, he walked to the puppy, and then bent down to scratch him on his chin. The little guy wagged his tail eagerly and looked up at Dave with pure, innocent joy. Dave's mouth started curling into a smile as he caught a whiff of his puppy breath. He was starting to soften a little.

Dave looked up at the rescue personnel and asked, "How'd he end up here?"

"Someone found the poor thing abandoned on the side of the road near the lake and brought him here."

"What's his name?"

With twinkling eyes and a proud smile, "We just named him Sunny."

Dave's eyes widened in disbelief and then started to well up with tears.

Katie gasped as her own watering eyes moved from Dave to Rachel.

"I can't believe it!" Rachel was stunned.

They were all thinking the same thought without actually saying it out loud: It's meant to be.

Dave reeled everyone back to the world of responsibility. He insisted, "Well, we have to go so I can make my bike ride. Let's all just think about it."

On the drive to Dave's friend's house, each of the three were wrapped in their own thoughts about two special dogs named Sunny. After pulling into the driveway and putting the car in park, Dave and Katie got out to unload the bike. Katie took over the driver's seat and Rachel climbed up front to the passenger's side.

Dave leaned into the window and looked at his girls, "Go get our dog."

The girls squealed with excitement. Katie turned to Dave and gave him a loving quick kiss on the lips.

Dave returned home later that day and was greeted at the door by a happy and grateful young dog. "Hey, boy! Welcome to your new home."

After getting to know the cute fella better, Dave offered a suggestion to his daughter and future wife. "As cool as it is that the shelter named this cute guy Sunny, I think it will be too hard to keep that name. What if we name him Mujjy?"

Mujjy—pronounced 'moo-zhee'—is a word that Dave and his close group of friends made up meaning "awesome" or "cool".

"Love it, Dad! Love you, too." Rachel gave her dad a big hug.

Later that year, Mujjy was the ring bearer in Dave and Katie's wedding. The family believes that Mujjy is truly a gift from Sunny.

7

BIG HEARTS GROWING BIGGER IS PAWSIBLE

Since their newlywed years, Jim and Irene have always had a Labrador by their side. Each one lived long, happy lives of 12 to 13 years, and each one held a very special place in both their hearts. Georgie Girl was no different. Losing this beautiful 13-year old Lab was devastating for Jim and Irene.

Irene noticed the hole that Georgie Girl left in her husband's heart was making him stir crazy. It had only been two weeks, but she determined he needed a dog. Only a dog—a special dog— would ease him.

Still grieving over the loss of Georgie Girl herself, Irene didn't feel quite ready for a new family member. Even so, something compelled her to look on the Los Angeles Animal Shelter (LAAS) website one Friday afternoon at work. She came across Layla and emailed her photo to Jim, who was working from home. There was something about this girl that Irene was drawn to. It was an inexplicable feeling.

Displaying some resistance to the idea, Jim called his wife after looking at Layla's online profile. "She's a real runt for a Labrador."

"Well, maybe you could just go to the shelter and meet her and see what you think?" Irene gently suggested.

"I suppose I could do that. I'm not sure about her, but I'll head over there now."

When Jim arrived at Layla's kennel, he found the eight month old puppy curled up in a ball of fear in the corner. She was a true runt-of-the-litter Yellow Labrador Retriever mix keeping a low profile in a kennel she shared with four large, rambunctious Pit Bulls. The way she cowered made her appear even smaller than she was.

Stepping away from the kennel, Jim reached into his pocket for his phone and walked toward the exit. "Irene, she's trying to disappear in the corner. I don't know about her. She's real small. We've always had big dogs "

Irene was determined. Her heart wanted to save this dog. "Jim, she's so cute in her picture! She looks like a little convict behind bars. You really need to get her out of there. She's only eight months old. Curiosity is written all over her face! We can give her a great life."

Suddenly convinced and confident, Jim agreed with his wife. They should adopt her. As he walked back to Layla's kennel, he saw a woman leading her around on a leash.

"Excuse me, ma'am? I would like to adopt that dog."

"Oh, well, she's mine now. I just signed for her."

"Are you with a rescue organization?"

"Yes, a Labrador rescue."

"So, you need to go find a home for her, and I'm a home right here. What can I do to convince you that I want this dog and would give her a great home?"

They went outside and the woman interviewed Jim for over an hour to make sure he and his wife could provide a good home for Layla. As she asked him question after question about their home, yard, children, and dog ownership history, it dawned on Jim that this dog already had a piece of his heart.

Finally, the rescue worker was satisfied that Jim and Irene would provide Layla with a wonderful home. She wished him and Layla the best.

It was near closing time on a Friday. Jim completed all the paperwork and paid the adoption fee. He was excited and ready to bring this girl to her new home.

The shelter worker delivered some disappointing news. "Sir, we require that all of our adopted animals be spayed or neutered and microchipped before they leave the shelter."

"Okay, that's understandable."

"The thing is that we do not do medical procedures over the weekend. She will have to be spayed and microchipped on Monday. We'll need to hold her here until then."

Jim was struck with worry. He hated the idea of her spending three more stressful nights at the shelter. All he could do was hope she would be okay.

After a restless weekend, Jim arrived at the shelter at the earliest moment he could pick up Layla to bring her to her forever home. He noticed right away she was off. It was more than side effects of having just been spayed. She was listless—in a trance-like state. Shortly after arriving home, he called his wife at work. "Irene, I'm taking her to the vet. Something's wrong. She won't eat. She won't do anything. She just keeps staring blankly—at nothing."

Frustration accompanied Jim's worry. He knew that the longer any dog stayed in a shelter, the greater the chances they would catch a virus or other illness. Sure enough, during those extra three days that Layla had to stay at the shelter, she became gravely ill with a parasite.

Getting her well was not inexpensive. A vet visit and $1000 later, Layla was on the road to recovery. Thankfully, antibiotics did the trick. She returned to full health in a couple of days.

It took Layla less time to adapt to her new home than it did to get over the virus. She was thrilled to be a part of this wonderful family. There was a lot of activity to keep her curious mind entertained. Irene and Jim were in the midst of remodeling their home, and Layla was certain that all of the construction workers were her personal toys.

Most of the construction workers were Hispanic. They called to her and played with her in Spanish "Aquí, perro! Vienen aquí." (Here, dog! Come here.) Layla was soon a bilingual canine and thought her name was Perro.

Shortly before adopting Layla, Jim quit his job and started working full-time from home as a travel writer. From the moment she entered their lives, Layla and Jim spent a lot of time together. After a few weeks, his doubts about her still lingered and surfaced from time to time. "She's just so small, Irene."

Jim's wife cringed. Irene adored this girl. She silently hoped this hang-up of his would disintegrate with time. Deep inside she knew it had nothing to do with Layla and everything to do with letting go of Georgie Girl.

One day, Irene came home and noticed that Jim was in a funny mood. "What's going on, sweetie?"

He sighed with unabashed love, "Today she got me."

"That's wonderful, Jim! What happened?"

"Nothing in particular. She just … . She took over the day. She's my dog." His eyes twinkled with pride.

Irene was over the moon with happiness.

Jim and Layla's bond continued to grow. When Jim wasn't traveling for work, he and Layla were together 24 hours a day, seven days a week. They were a team. Everywhere Jim went, Layla was sure to follow, unless Jim was writing. During work time, Layla preferred to hang outside and chat it up with the neighbors. Jim could hear people call out, "Hello, Layla!" She knew every dog and person in the neighborhood. When the pair went for walks, many neighbors didn't know who Jim was, but they sure knew the dog by his side, "Oh, you're Layla's dad!"

Layla also quickly grew attached to Irene. When Jim was on his travels, Layla was happy to get Irene all to herself. She didn't hesitate to make herself comfortable on Jim's side of the bed when nighttime arrived. In the morning, she threw herself onto Jim's pillow, laid on her back and wriggled about. "Aw, sweetie! Good morning. Taking in your dad's essence again, I see!" Irene gave her girl a nice belly rub as they both got in their morning giggles.

Layla

Irene had a loveseat that she sat on when reading or watching TV. Layla enjoyed sitting right by her side to keep her company. If Irene wasn't sitting in her spot, Layla would take it over and stare at Irene as if to say, "Come, Mom. Sit here with me, please."

"Oh, Layla! Fine. I'm coming. You are such a slut for attention!" Irene teased.

A smile swept across Layla's face as she scooted over and made room for her mom.

Layla knew just how to communicate to ensure she got what she wanted. When it was time to go for a walk, she adamantly jumped onto her back legs and stood by the cupboard where her leash was kept. If Jim didn't take the hint, then the feisty girl began head butting him.

When Irene and Jim had company visiting and Layla wanted to go to bed, she didn't hesitate to let them know she would like the guests to leave so she could curl up to get her beauty sleep. She went right up to the guests, looked at them, and then walked to and waited at the front door.

Guests looked at Irene and Jim with a laugh, "I guess that's our cue to leave! Did you train her to do that?"

They both joined the laughter and Jim blurted out, "No! It's all her."

Irene blushed, "Really. All her!"

Layla came a long way from that cowering, timid girl trying to disappear in the corner of a shelter kennel. In fact, she became a bit of a local celebrity. Not only was she one of the most popular dogs in the neighborhood, but she also had a fan base from some stints as a guest columnist for a local online newspaper, Studio City Patch. With a little help from her dad, she filled in a few times for Heidi "Boo" Feldstein, a beloved German Shepherd and local columnist. Layla's writing portfolio also included articles published in the Christian Science Monitor and Los Angeles Times.

As a travel writer, Jim journeyed across the globe. Irene, co-founder of The Society of Women Adventurers, often accompanied him. Although Layla didn't join her dad and mom on their travels, she was well-cared-for while they were away. Upon the couple's return, she was known to put up a little attitude, but she got over it, and the three enjoyed their own adventures together.

As long as Layla's escapades didn't involve water, she was a happy camper. The three once went on a walk by the marina. Admiring the water, Jim said to his lovely wife, "Irene, she is the only Labrador I've ever known that doesn't like water."

"She just doesn't like getting her pads wet."

Suddenly, a flock of sea gulls took off over the water. Completely focused on the birds, Layla dashed into the water for the first time in her life. Shock and dismay swept over her face when she realized she was not on land—and, wet! "What have I done?"

With each stroke, her doggy paddle became more confident. She started swimming in circles, "I can do this! I can do this!"

Bright smiles spread across her mom and dad's faces. "Oh, Jim. Look at her. She didn't know she could swim."

"She is hating being wet."

"That's for sure!" They both laughed and smiled admirably at their tenacious girl as she made her way out of the water.

Thankful to be on solid ground, Layla ran to them and wildly shook her coat as she arrived at their feet. "Now, you're wet, too."

She sat, looked up at her beloved humans, and grinned sweetly.

Layla with Jim and Irene

In June 2015, Layla took her last breath after cancer presented itself in her 13-year-old body. Jim and Irene were left heartbroken over the loss of their dear friend. After six weeks of crying, they could not go on another moment without a dog. The great love and tremendous loss of Layla fueled their overwhelming need to adopt again.

They welcomed Gracie, a beautiful one-year-old Golden Retriever-Spaniel mix, into their family. Filled with great pride, while still grieving for his beloved Layla, Jim said, "Gracie has very big paws to fill, but we both know she will do it."

Just as Layla was a tribute to Georgie Girl, Gracie is a tribute to Layla. With each dog, Jim and Irene's hearts just keep getting bigger.

8

BAD LUCK TURNING INTO GOOD LUCK IS PAWSIBLE

Sometimes, unlucky is lucky. For Lisa, a leaky faucet was a blessing in disguise. Her neighbor, Bob, was a plumber. A few days after he made the repairs, Lisa walked to his house to pay the bill. His wife was sitting outside enjoying another nice November day that Southern California delivered.

"Hi, Lisa! How are you? How are the dogs?"

Lisa's eyes turned sad. "Well, actually, I'm dogless. I had to put Joe down in March and Sophie in September."

"Oh, dear. I'm so sorry. They were such beautiful Boxers. Weren't they brother and sister?"

"Yes, they were litter mates. I really, really miss them."

"I bet you do. When you're ready, maybe you'll adopt, again?"

"Yes, for sure. I started looking a little here and there. I checked out petfinder.com and a Boxer rescue. None of them grabbed me. I'll find them when the time is right."

"You definitely will, dear. I'll keep my eyes open for you, too."

"Thank you." Lisa's smile offered sincerity with a melancholy heart.

Two weeks later, Bob knocked on Lisa's door.

"Hi, Bob."

"Hey, Lisa. You were the first person my wife and I thought of when we found out about these two dogs. Have a look." He showed her a photo of two Boxer puppies.

"Oh, they're adorable! Whose are they?"

"Someone just left them in front of the SPCA. The guy renting that property from me in Hawthorne found them. The place is just four doors down from the shelter and he kept hearing cars squealing on their brakes. When he went out there, he saw these two running around. Cars were dodging them left and right."

"Oh, my gosh!"

"Whoever dumped them didn't bother to bring them inside or tie them to the door to keep them safe. Awful. Just awful. Anyway, my renter and his friend were able to rescue them. I met them when I went to collect the rent."

"They're beautiful!"

"Oh, they certainly are. He doesn't want to bring them to SPCA because he thinks they're meant to be together. They're siblings. A boy and a girl. He's not sure two Boxers would get adopted together."

"How old are they?"

"Not sure. Maybe about 8 months or so. They need a home." Bob smiled large and winked at Lisa.

Lisa grinned back. "I will go meet them."

Lisa went to the tenant's home the next day after work. It was located in an industrial area. The man who rescued the dogs had a little house in front and a big auto shop in the back. The yard was a small square of grass. He already had a dog. Two young Boxers put him over capacity.

"Hey. You must be Lisa."

"Yes, I heard you had a couple of cute Boxers here!" Lisa was grinning from ear to ear.

"I sure do! Come on in. Let me introduce you."

Lucy (left) listens intently to Oscar sharing a secret

Lisa took one look at them and her heart melted. "That's it. Done."

"Congratulations!"

Lisa pulled into the garage with her new brood in the back seat. Super excited, it didn't occur to her that she should close the garage door. She opened the back car door and led the male to her fenced backyard. When she returned to the car, the female had made a run for it. Panic swept over Lisa. She didn't even have a name for the dog, yet. She ran up and down the street repeatedly yelling, "Dog! Dog! Come back here! Here, dog! C'mon, girl!"

Oscar and Lucy with Lisa

With the help of a neighbor with a fence around her entire house, they managed to corner the pup. Filled with relief, Lisa sat next to the girl and pet her. "Oh, my goodness. You really gave me a scare!" After catching her breath, she carried the Boxer pup home.

Later that evening, Lisa went out to dinner with a friend. Being that she had had two Boxers before, Lisa's home was well equipped for this pair. She even had a doggy door. She decided to leave the dogs in the backyard. Upon her return, Lisa discovered the duo sitting on the sofa. She was impressed. They figured out the doggy door! However, the guilty looks on their faces had her concerned. What did they get into? She looked around. Everything was intact.

"It's okay, you two. You're not in trouble. You are welcome to be inside here. This is your home!" She sat down between them.

"This must be confusing for you. This is the third home you've had in just four days. Let's make it official. You need names. For you, mister, you are Oscar. You remind me of Oscar Madison from 'The Odd Couple.' Or, even Oscar the Grouch. You might look intimidating to some, but you are just a big softie, aren't you, sweetheart?" He licked her face.

Oscar giving Lisa a big kiss

"And, you, Miss Troublemaker. You are going to give me a lot of laughs, aren't you? You're a crazy, mischievous comedienne like Lucille Ball." She jumped off the couch and chased her tail.

"Lucy it is!"

That week, Lisa took them to the vet. They got all their shots and microchipped. She also set up dog walking services for them for when she was away at work. With inordinate amounts of energy, Lucy and Oscar needed a mid-day walk. She decided they needed a massage once a week to help keep them calm and relaxed. Their dog walker, Allyson, was a licensed pet massage therapist. So, why not? They deserved it!

On one of their daily after-work walks, the trio ran into Bob. "Looks like your pack is doing well, Lisa."

"They are! Thank you so much. I'm so grateful to you. I can't believe how perfect the timing was when they came into my life. I had a little extra money at the end of each month after losing Joe and Sophie. I was debating whether to do home improvements or get dogs, and then these two came along. My house is a little worn down, but I have Oscar and Lucy!"

"They deserve a wonderful home and I knew you could provide it. A perfect match! Did they settle in quickly?"

"Well, actually, it took about six months for them to truly come out of their shell and get comfortable. I think they were backyard dogs and weren't allowed inside the house."

"Why do you say that?"

"Well, I have a doggy door, so they can go in and out as they please. Anytime I come home and they are inside, they have such guilty looks on their faces. It's like they think I caught them doing something bad."

"Oh, wow. Yeah, that makes sense."

"It's a little upsetting. Why have a dog if you're not going to make them part of the family?"

"Now, they have a family. You are their family. You rescued them."

"Some days it feels more like they rescued me. Especially after a rough day at work. When I come home, they are there to just listen. I tell them, 'You wouldn't believe what happened at work today!' Then, I ask them about their day, 'So, did you catch any squirrels?'"

Bob laughed at Lisa's animated description. "Do they ever answer?"

"In their own way. They both just make me laugh. Oscar is a big goofball. And, Lucy? Lucy runs the house. She just lets Oscar and I live there with her. I love them both so much. We *are* family."

9

RAGS TO RICHES IS PAWSIBLE

In Bozeman, Montana, a nine-year-old boy received a Black Labrador puppy as a gift from a friend. Pets were not allowed in the apartment building where he lived with his parents. He knew that but was desperate to keep the dog.

He stuffed the young pup into his backpack. Once inside the apartment, he surreptitiously bypassed his parents and headed straight to his bedroom. Quietly closing the door behind him, he went to the closet and sat inside. As if unwrapping a longed-for Christmas present, he ecstatically unzipped the backpack. Out jumped the wriggly puppy.

"Welcome home, doggy!" He whispered with excitement. "I will take good care of you. Oh, gosh. You need a name."

Without much thought, he blurted, "Blackie. I'm going to call you Blackie." The young boy hugged the young dog adoringly. For weeks, he managed to keep his secret. He snuck food and water into the dark closet where Blackie spent every moment of each day. When nighttime fell, the boy was able to sneak him outside for fresh air. Blackie never saw the light of day.

Hiding a growing, active puppy became more and more difficult. When the boy's parents discovered their son had been hiding a dog right beneath their noses, they brought the sweet, young Lab to Heart of the Valley, a no-kill shelter. Blackie was admitted as a cruelty hold.

Although the boy's heart may have been in the right place, the puppy's health had suffered during his time living in a closet. Blackie's eyes were constantly dilated and took on a dark gray color resembling smoke. He was renamed Smokey by the shelter workers.

The compassionate team at Heart of the Valley Animal Shelter quickly recognized that Smokey needed to be socialized to become eligible for adoption. Up to this point, he had led a life of isolation. That was about to change with the help of a foster.

The woman who volunteered to foster the young Black Lab lived on a ranch with horses, cats, and other dogs. Her young grandchildren visited every day. Smokey was exposed to wide open spaces and made many new friends. It was a whole new, big, bright world!

During his two-month stay on the ranch, the young Black Lab's eyes returned to normal and his happy-go-lucky personality emerged. His foster mom renamed him again. Jake. This time the name stuck.

When Jake was ready for a forever home, his foster mom said a bittersweet goodbye and returned him to Heart of the Valley Shelter. Everyone there agreed that Jake would be adopted quickly.

Monique and her family lived in Southern California but had property in Montana. During one of their many trips to Big Sky Country, they stopped at Heart of the Valley Shelter to see the dogs for adoption. "Mom! Dad! Come look at this boy. He's so cute!" Monique's oldest daughter, Christina, was completely enamored by Jake.

"He's adorable, sweetie!" Monique knelt down to say hello and let him sniff the back of her hand. Her youngest daughter, Alessandra, followed her mom's lead and giggled when Jake's wet nose pressed against the back of her hand.

A sign caught Monique's eye and she pointed to it. "Oh, no. Looks like he's not available for adoption. He's being dewormed."

Disappointment swept across Christina's face. Monique felt and showed the same pang. Seeing the sad looks on his daughter and wife's faces, Greg felt compelled to investigate. "Let's go ask somebody just to make sure."

A kind shelter worker looked through Jake's paperwork. "I have good news. There were two other dogs in pens in the same area as Jake's pen. The sign applied to them, not Jake. Jake is definitely available to adopt, and I would recommend getting an application in fast."

"No wonder no one has snatched him up, yet. Nobody realized he was available." Monique shared a smile of excitement with Christina.

"Would you like to submit an application to adopt him?" The shelter worker asked as she placed the paperwork before them.

"Absolutely!" Greg was excited, too.

"We need 24 hours to process your application. If you come back tomorrow about the same time, we will let you know whether you are a good match for Jake and approved to adopt him."

When they returned the next day, they learned that not only were they approved, but six other people had submitted applications after they did. Luck was on their side.

Joy beamed from Christina's face. Alessandra was giddy. They had a one-and-a-half-year-old Yellow Lab at home, and had recently lost their old Yellow Lab, Churchill. The time felt right to welcome a new family member into their home.

The shelter worker walked back to Jake's pen with Monique and Christina. Filled with tremendous excitement, Christina spoke to Jake, "Hi, Jake! Guess what? You can come home with us. What do you think about that?"

Jake with Monique

Jake wagged his tail in full agreement. Twenty-four hours later, he was on a road trip to his new home in Manhattan Beach, California. Jake adjusted well and quickly to his new laidback beach lifestyle, and to his new canine brother, Luke.

Monique noticed one peculiarity about Jake. She pointed it out to her oldest daughter, "I think Jakey is afraid of the dark."

"Really? Why?"

"He always has to be touching me in the dark. He sleeps with his head on me or hits me with his nose to make sure I'm there."

"Oh, yeah! And, you know how he goes nutso every time he's in the car?"

"Yes, dark and tight spaces really do freak him out."

"Is he claustrophobic, Mom?"

"I think that's a good diagnosis, sweetie. If I were trapped in a closet for a month, I think I would be, too."

"Me, too. That would be awful."

"All we can do is keep working with him and helping him feel comfortable going for car rides. You're a good, sweet boy, aren't you, Jake?" Monique turned and gave him some pets, and then tossed his ball. He playfully pounced after it and continued following it around the room.

For six years, Jake and Luke bonded. Jake adored his older brother, who showed him the ropes to being a good dog in a good home. Jake was the roly poly puppy that followed his older, mature brother around, while Luke let him. Happy dogs with happy lives.

The family was devastated when Luke was diagnosed with osteosarcoma, an aggressive bone cancer. Monique chose to have Luke put down at home surrounded by the ones who loved him most.

The veterinarian gently asked, "Monique, would you like Jake to be present, too?"

With sorrowful eyes, Monique thoughtfully replied, "Yes, we would. I think it's really important for him to understand Luke's passing, instead of him being taken away never to return. They're close. They're brothers."

"I think that's a lovely gift." The vet was touched.

When the time came, Jake got very quiet. Each family member said their goodbyes. There was silence. Silence and tears. As the vet and vet technician took Luke's body out the front door, Jake watched attentively. He continued watching the front door long after they were gone.

The next day, Jake walked through the house and smelled all the areas where Luke had been. It was as if he suddenly understood. With acceptance, his personality switched. He went from being a young, crazy puppy to a wise, mature dog.

A few months after Luke's passing, Monique and Alessandra attended a pet adoption event at a local pet store. It was Valentine's Day 2012.

"Oh, my gosh, Mom! Isn't this guy so cute?"

"He's really skinny, but that face!"

Rover Rescue was the animal rescue hosting the adoption event. One of the volunteers approached to offer the young Chocolate Lab's story. "Hi! I see you're getting acquainted with Charlie."

"Yes, he's adorable. So thin, though. What happened?"

"He was found on the streets starving to death. Animal control picked him up and brought him to the Carson Shelter. He spent almost a month there. Rover Rescue kept their eyes on him. When he didn't get adopted, we worked to find a foster so we could pull him out of the shelter. He's put on some weight in his foster home, but he needs to gain some more."

"Poor guy. He's so lucky you guys found him. You do such selfless work."

"It's a lot of teamwork. Charlie is living with his second foster, now. His original foster family started painting their home and was worried with all the hired help going in and out of the house that Charlie might escape. Charlie's current foster is the founder of Rover Rescue. He has a lot of dogs and discovered that Charlie really does well with the company and companionship. When he's left alone he tends to be destructive."

"We have another dog he could be pals with!" Alessandra looked at her mom with pleading, excited eyes.

"I should tell you that we do have another family interested in adopting him, but the woman and her son do not have another dog. Also, the son is off to college next year. We really think he needs a home with another dog and more human companionship."

Sharing the same good, excited feeling about this young Chocolate Lab as her daughter, Monique didn't hesitate to speak up, "We are definitely interested in adopting him. Our Black Lab at home really misses his brother, who passed away a few months ago. He and Charlie would make a great pair."

One interview and a house visit later, Charlie had a new, forever home. Jake happily shed his only-canine-child crown to take on the role of older sibling. He stepped into the shoes of his beloved brother, Luke, and kindly welcomed Charlie into the family. Charlie bonded with Jake immediately.

On Charlie's first night in his new home, he slept with his chin nuzzled on Monique's neck. He craved the security of a person, and Monique happily obliged.

A few months after Charlie was settled in, Monique met up with a friend. "How are things going? How's the new dog?"

"Things are good. Charlie is great! He and Jake are the best of friends. Charlie definitely doesn't like to be left alone. We tried it once and he barked nonstop."

"He's still adjusting, I'm sure."

"Yeah, that's a big part of it. He's a naturally curious dog and tends to get into a bit of mischief. The other day, I caught him on the dining room table helping himself to some food we hadn't cleared off."

Charlie with Monique

"Oh, no!" Her friend laughed and Monique joined in.

"He's also chewed up many bras!"

"He has a thing for women's undergarments, huh?" Monique's friend teased.

"Like I said, curious!" Monique smiled and sighed. "He's actually come a long way, though. His coat used to be prickly. Now, it's soft and silky. He put on that weight he needed to. I think there's a reason he was a stray. I think he was being mistreated and ran away from home."

"Why do you say that?"

"He's really afraid of some things. Like the fly swatter. He's terrified. He used to be afraid when I would pick him up. He would totally freeze. He's okay with it now. He knows I'll put him down gently. We've worked really hard to build trust with him. He still eats super fast. It's as if he's not sure whether he's going to get another meal."

"He's so lucky you adopted him."

"We are the lucky ones. He's been a good dog. As you know, this divorce …," Her voice trailed off when a lump rose in her throat. As her eyes welled up with tears, she looked up to prevent them from falling down her cheeks.

Her friend reached out to her hold her hand. Monique gave a quick smile and regained her composure. "It has been a really long, hard four years. The dogs have been there for us. Jake has been especially amazing. He's always there for me. He's like a therapy dog. I would do anything for that boy."

"Rescued dogs are the best support system. You save their life, and they save yours right back."

Monique was thoughtful, "You are so right about rescued dogs. I have to say, my adopted dogs have a true sense of appreciation and compassion. They have a really strong sense of trust. I think it comes from experiencing hard times."

"I totally agree. My adopted dog is just … grateful. Adopting is the way to go."

"It really is. I owned AKC bred Labs for years. I will never, ever buy a dog again. I will always adopt."

"As they say, you save two lives when you adopt from a shelter or rescue. The one you adopted, and the one who takes his place in the shelter."

"Charlie is a true rags-to-riches story. On December 29, 2011, he was in the Carson shelter surrounded by hundreds of other scared, homeless dogs, and laying on a cold cement floor with pee and poop on it for a bed. A year later, on December 29, 2012, he was in a cozy home in Manhattan Beach sound asleep on a Tempur-Pedic bed with a blankie wrapped around him."

"I love happy endings!"

"Me, too. The shelter workers and animal rescue volunteers are the ones that create these happy endings. Such incredible, selfless work. These wonderful people give abused and abandoned animals their first glimpse into human kindness. Most have never experienced it, so they're terrified of humans."

"I don't know how they do it. They work tirelessly to make them adoptable for us."

"I truly respect all of the hard work of rescue organizations. I received a great gift. They gave me that gift. They're amazing!"

Monique returned home feeling extra grateful for her rescued dogs. As she walked through the door, she was greeted with uproarious bellows and heavy-duty tail wags of two excited young Labs.

"Hi, Jakey! Hi, Charlie!" She returned their love with simultaneous belly rubs and laughed as they wriggled on the floor with happy tongues hanging out of their wide grins. "You two are the best! I love you."

Jake and Charlie

10

A GUARDIAN ANGEL IS PAWSIBLE

On September 21, 2008, Filbert, Chance, and I made a weekend trip to Bakersfield to see my brother, his wife, and their two young boys. My mom and stepdad were also there. The whole gang went to a nearby park to play baseball and exercise the dogs.

Moments after Filbert, Chance, and I stepped paws and foot on the paved path through the park, an adorable, extremely gregarious, young dog sprinted to greet us. He approached Filbert first. Filbert's butterfly ears perked up and his busy tail wagged excitedly. The two came nose-to-nose and exchanged a sweet smooch.

The little dude moved toward Chance. Tails were wagging fast and curiously. I kneeled down thinking he would come right to me because he was so friendly with my boys. Wrong! He darted instantly. When it came to humans, this canine was definitely a fan of the three-feet distance rule.

The young dog looked like a fox and found Chance to be the perfect playmate. They chased each other for 90 minutes in the park. Chance gladly welcomed the shenanigans his new friend delivered. Filbert was 13 years young, but not as spunky as he used to be. He opted out of the antics.

As the two played, I walked around the park asking everyone if the fox look-a-like was theirs. My question was received with pitying "Nos" and shakes of the head.

I continued to attempt to gain his trust but also continued to fail. When it came time to leave, the dog was still highly skeptical of me and my human family. He thought Filbert was pretty cool. If he could talk, I'm certain he would have told Chance, "Dog, you're the bomb!"

The small mutt followed Chance five blocks back to my brother's home. It offered us the perfect opportunity to lead him to an enclosed area. Chance and I walked into my brother's fenced backyard. As the little fox followed, my stepdad quickly closed the gate behind us.

It took 20 minutes of slow, gentle determination, but eventually I was able to corner and grab hold of the small guy. He was petrified. He wriggled and writhed in an effort to break free, but I held him tight and close to my chest. Calmly, I sang to him as I rocked him. It took time, but eventually he calmed down. When he did, I took a close look at him.

The young dog was wearing a collar. It was so tight that I couldn't twist it. In fact, it was pinching his skin as if he had grown since it was first put on. I removed it. There were no tags attached.

After taking his photo, I created a flyer and posted it all over the neighborhood. I took him for a walk asking anyone I saw if they recognized him. I also knocked on several doors. No luck.

During our walk, I noticed his oddly bent tail. Could dogs break their tail?

"What happened to you, doggy?" I asked out loud in hopes of an answer that could not come.

Something in my gut told me this dog had been abandoned. It was happening all over America. The huge housing market crash of 2007 and 2008 forced people to bail on homes they could no longer afford. The worst part was that many were also leaving their pets behind as if they were a possession that could just be discarded and forgotten.

My heart hurt for this emotionally and physically broken animal that found us in the park. I appropriately named him Parker, and took him home with me, an hour drive south to Santa Clarita, California. I didn't have any intention of keeping him. I wanted to help him stay safe. I had never come across such a terrified dog. He was afraid of everyone and everything, except Filbert and Chance. Did I mention how much he adored Chance?

Sometimes, you pick a dog. Sometimes, a dog picks you. Other times, a dog picks your dog. Parker picked Chance. This became undisputedly clear over the following weeks.

I placed a Found Dog report with Bakersfield Animal Control Center, and called back every day for a week. No one was looking for Parker. During the same week, I took him to my trusted veterinarian for a physical.

"Who have we got here?" The vet asked.

"He's a stray who followed us home from the park."

"Has he been scanned for a microchip?"

"Not yet."

She moved the scanner back and forth over his coat. "Nope. No chip."

I was not surprised. "Can you check him out and get him up-to-date on shots?"

"Absolutely. What breeds are we thinking he is?"

"Well, I think Corgi and Chihuahua."

She nodded. "I can see that."

"What do you think is up with his tail? See how it's sort of bent? Is it broken?"

"It could be a fracture. If it were closer to the base, I would be concerned, but it's closer to the end of his tail. It should heal on its own. "

"Oh, good. Okay. I'll keep an eye on it. How old do you think he is?"

She lifted his gum to look at his teeth. "I would put him at two years old. He has quite an overbite!" She smiled.

"Yes, it's pretty cute." I returned the smile and laughed.

While we were there, she got a fecal sample and delivered the results. "This is really strange, but he does have a bacterial infection. The weird part is that it is a bacteria that is normally only found in rabbits."

I sat there mystified, and then it suddenly occurred to me. "Oh, my gosh. I noticed he is constantly grazing the grass when we go on walks. There are tons of rabbits. Do you think he's been living on rabbit poop?"

"That explains it! I'm sure he scrounged for any food source he could, if he was living on the streets."

Over the next few weeks, Parker's tail lost its crooked bend and found its natural, happy curl. With the help of antibiotics, he rid himself of the bacterial infection. Physically, he was all good. Emotionally, he was still a mess, but he was learning to trust me.

For nearly two months, life was pretty hectic with three dogs: an abandoned and abused puppy, a rambunctious teenager, and a spoiled old man. That all changed November 15, 2008.

In the early morning, as he lay sleeping against my arm, Filbert had a stroke. After it happened, he was disoriented and had difficulty breathing. At the time, I had no idea what was wrong. I was worried but calm.

On the ride to the vet, he sat on my lap in the driver's seat and stuck his little head out the window as he always did to catch the breeze. When we arrived, the veterinarian told me they would put him on oxygen, and I could pick him up later that day. Filbert looked at me with scared eyes. His little tongue sweetly peeped out between his lips. I kissed his forehead and promised, "I will be right back, Fil-B. I love you."

About an hour later, I received an urgent call from the vet. Filbert had gone into cardiac arrest and was in critical condition. I immediately left home to get back to him.

There were wildfires surrounding the Santa Clarita Valley that day. As a result, the freeways were closed. I raced through the city side streets from one end of town to the other to get to Filbert. Along the way, I hit every single red light. Every stop was lost time. Every stop was agony.

When I finally arrived at the vet's office, I sprinted through the door. As I did, Filbert's veterinarian had just walked into the reception area from the back. She looked at me across the waiting room with sorrowful eyes and shook her head. I was too late.

"No!" I cried out in despair. Sympathetic eyes watched me as I ran across the waiting room. With great compassion, the vet escorted me to a room where Filbert's lifeless body laid on an exam table.

"May I please have a moment alone with him?"

"Of course. Take your time."

I felt as though failed him. I didn't make it in time, and now he was gone. I apologized over and over and over again. I told Filbert how much I loved him. He had been there for me through thick and thin for thirteen years. What would I do without him?

I stayed by Filbert's side as long as the vet let me. She eventually came in and gently led me out of the room. I left devastated and felt empty. I couldn't feel his presence anywhere. I was not there for him when he passed. Now, his spirit was lost. I prayed he would find me.

Over the next couple of days, I received many kind condolences. My friend, Ellen, thoughtfully offered, "Maybe Parker was an angel sent from God to help you through the loss of Filbert?"

His arrival in our lives was certainly coincidental timing. I thought about the several pairs of designer shoes he destroyed, the baseboards he chewed away, the arm of the chair he ate, and all the toys he destuffed or decapitated. No, Parker was not the angel here, but she was definitely on to something.

Three days after Filbert's death, we practiced our daily treat ritual before I headed out the door to work.

"Chance, sit." Obedient, as always, I rewarded him with a treat after he sat.

"Parker, sit." I expected him to do his clueless puppy dance for the thousandth time. Two months had gone by since he entered my home and he still wouldn't sit on command.

This time, something magical happened.

Filbert appeared.

With a gentle grace, he lingered over Parker. Filbert's presence was strong, and Parker listened to it intently. As he did, a calmness overtook him, and he sweetly sat exactly as Filbert used to sit. As soon as he did, Filbert's spirit swept over me and made its way home into my heart. He was no longer lost. He found me. He found peace. My cup runneth over when I realized that Parker now had an angel watching over him.

Filbert and Parker are so different, yet there are still days when Parker does something exactly the way Filbert did. Sometimes it's in the way he sits. Other times it's the way he runs through the grass with a happy-go-lucky smile. Those are moments when I'm reminded that Fil-B, my Happy Papi, is still there, reaching out and speaking to me through Parker.

Dogs never really leave us. Just like Monroe, Filbert is with me forever.

11

STOPPING ABUSE AND NEGLECT IS PAWSIBLE

A woman, we'll call her Jane, moved to a new city to start a new job and was invited to a new co-worker's home. "Jane" is not this woman's real name. It has been changed to respect this courageous person's privacy. Upon arriving at her co-worker's home, she met their dog. It was a Beagle. A healthy, normal-looking Beagle. This fact made her horrifying discovery even more perplexing.

Jane was startled and deeply concerned when she came upon a young, full-grown, yet severely emaciated, Great Dane crammed into a metal animal crate inside her co-worker's garage. Not sure what to do, but compelled to take action, Jane somehow managed to get the frail canine out of her crate and took a photo with her camera phone. The dog's name was Lucy. The situation was disgraceful. Jane was afraid.

Jane was afraid of jeopardizing her job, but even more afraid for this precious canine's life. Lucy could barely lift her head. Barely. Her hunched stance made it clear that she had spent her life to this point confined in a cage. Unsure how to handle this situation, Jane posted the photo of the horrifically maltreated Merlequin Great Dane on Facebook.

The photograph instantly drew responses of outrage and wrath. People vented and screamed, "My god, this is horrible!" and "Who would do such a despicable thing?" Most of the comments were filled with so much hatred and anger that both Jane and the neglectful owner became quite frightened.

Catherine came across the alarming photo on her Facebook newsfeed. Instantly, she knew she had to save this dying dog. Great Danes were Catherine's heart and soul. For 30 years, she had cared for and loved this giant, yet delicate and sensitive breed. Lucy's gentle, scared soul screamed out for help to Catherine through the computer screen. Lucy's plea became Catherine's mission. She would stop at nothing to save this girl. She had to be smart about it. Lucy's life was on the line.

Although overflowing with rage, Catherine knew impulsive, scathing words would not get her one inch closer to Lucy. She had to rise above berating the owner's appalling and unforgiveable treatment of this beautiful, gentle creature. Succumbing to the feeding frenzy of hatred would only build fear in the abusive owner, which could result in her lashing out on Lucy. Catherine took a kind and thoughtful approach. In a direct email to Jane on Facebook, she calmly explained with utmost sincerity why she would love to adopt Lucy and would be able to provide her with tender, attentive care that her sensitive breed needs. Heartfelt emotion flowed from her fingertips onto the keyboard as she typed. Her words came across genuine, knowledgeable and, most importantly, calm. Catherine wrote:

"I have extensive experience with the breed. I have two other Danes, a large yard and a heart full of love to give."

She shared photographs of her two beloved Harlequin Great Danes, Maggie and Bodhi, and then followed up with two more emails. Catherine expressed that she was more than willing to apply to adopt Lucy from a rescue if one was involved in negotiations to have her released.

Bursting at the seams with a mix of rage and worry, Catherine had an overwhelming urge to run to Lucy, but where would she go? The only clue Catherine had about Lucy's location was that she was "somewhere in Orange County." All she could do was wait. Time moved torturously slow.

Finally, the phone rang. It was Jane with a message from the dog owner, who realized how many people were angry with her and that chances were high that she would go to jail if she kept the starving Great Dane. The dog owner told Jane, "I might be interested in that lady maybe taking Lucy." She knew she had to get rid of the dog.

Soon after speaking with Jane, Catherine spoke directly with the abusive owner. It was surreal. As they spoke, rage simmered inside Catherine. Her gut screamed, "HOW COULD YOU DO THIS TO YOUR DOG?"

More determined than ever, Catherine's exterior remained cool, and she did not let one ounce of anger show. Instead, she put on a blasé show—as if the entire situation was no big deal. It was the only way to get this woman to surrender this precious being. Catherine said to her, "Great Danes are hard to handle. It's a hard breed because they're so large, but I've had them my entire life. If you'd like, I can take her so that you don't have to deal with her."

The woman was receptive. Catherine went on, "I'll come over to your house and get her."

Sternly and sharply, the woman replied, "No. We will bring her to you."

It was clear to Catherine that this woman did not want her to know where she lived. She wanted no trail connecting her abusive acts to this dying dog.

On New Year's Eve 2010, the woman arrived at Catherine's door with her husband to deliver Lucy. Catherine tried with all her might to conceal her shock and dismay. Lucy was a walking skeleton. She got lost for a moment in Lucy's soft, sweet eyes—one, the color of amber and the other, the color of a pale blue sky. Thank goodness this poor girl was finally here. A new year and a new life for Lucy.

Catherine's eyes shifted. She took quick note of the couple's appearance. These folks were not lacking for food. So, why? Why were they starving this dog? They had another dog at home they were feeding—that Beagle. It is not that hard to feed an animal—especially one as gentle as Lucy, who showed no signs of aggression. Ever. Just put food through the bars, for goodness sake. Feed her.

The couple followed Catherine inside her home with Lucy, whose walk was wobbly. In fact, Lucy could barely walk at all. Her body was weak. Her eyes were glazed over. She was unresponsive to touch. Lucy was disconnected from people, showing no affection. She was not afraid, but she was surrounded by a shield—completely zoned out.

There happened to be a couple of pieces of kibble on the floor, left behind by Catherine's two other Great Danes. Desperate for nourishment, a skeletal Lucy slowly bent down to eat them. The woman blurted, "Oh, what a piggy!"

It was all Catherine could do to contain herself. Determined to save this precious girl, she requested, "You want to just leave her? I will take care of her."

"Yeah."

Catherine asked, "What kind of food are you feeding her? It's easier for their digestion not to make a quick transition to a different kind of dog food."

The woman's response was disturbing. "I can't remember."

Catherine wondered if they were feeding her anything at all. She promptly requested the couple sign Lucy over to her. She wanted to be sure they could never come back and take her again. After signing papers, the apathetic pair took off without leaving an address or contact information, which left Catherine unable to press charges or file action against them. She really wanted to prevent them from being able to have animals, but, at least, Lucy was safe. Sick, sick Lucy. Would she pull through this?

Starved to the bone, Lucy was also infested with fleas and had chronic diarrhea. Her thin skin was marred by scratches, bumps, infections, and two distinct cigarette burns. Being confined inside a cage had taken its toll on her body. Forced to be curled in the same position day after day for over a year, the friction of her protruding bones against the hard surfaces of her cage resulted in painful sores. To top it off, Lucy had a severe case of splitting tail syndrome. Her tail was an open wound—raw and bleeding. It split at the end after repeatedly hitting it against the confines of her crate when she wagged it.

Catherine's first step toward saving Lucy was a visit to the vet. To cover all bases, the pair saw two trusted veterinarians. On a scale of 1 to 10—10 being excellent health—Lucy was a 2. Both vets told Catherine that Lucy probably would not have survived another week. She was a mere 68 pounds—essentially, the weight of her bones. Ideally, she should have been at least 110. Catherine rescued Lucy in the nick of time.

Even though Lucy was finally in extraordinary, loving hands, she was still in danger, high danger. The veterinarians were concerned about Lucy's organs shutting down one by one due to the long-term starvation. Lucy was also severely dehydrated. The week would be touch and go.

Lucy received fluids, electrolytes, and antibiotics. Catherine fed her small meals five times a day—an integral strategy for building up Lucy's digestive system. Feeding her too much too soon could be incredibly dangerous to her liver and kidneys. It's much like overworking a car engine that has not been turned on in many years. If you make it work too hard too soon, it dies.

In addition to the excellent care that Catherine provided, Lucy also received generous amounts of love and affection. Lucy's space was no longer limited. She had a giant bed cushion, upon which she could lie her head and stretch her entire body. At first, she would curl her long limbs into that oh-so-familiar ball position. Suddenly, her eyes would light up. She realized she had room—lots and lots of room to stretch as long and far as she wanted!

After four days, Lucy's body started morphing, and so did her personality. Yes, she was still thin and bony, but her caved in stomach was now a firm belly filled with nutritious sustenance. A layer of health was beginning to form over her ribs and hips. Not only was she more energetic, but she was also bright and alert. Still unsure of her new surroundings, yet wanting to express her gratitude, Lucy bestowed a gentle kiss upon Catherine's face. It was a beautiful sign and a far cry from the disoriented, feeble girl who arrived at Catherine's door less than a week ago.

Over the next couple of weeks, Lucy continued to gain weight. By Day 17 with Catherine, she was at 91 fabulous pounds. The one thing that was not improving was the tip of Lucy's tail. Catherine tried her best to keep it wrapped in hopes that it would heal and grow back, but it was to no avail. The cartilage was gone and skin would not cover the wound. The only solution was to have it docked.

Lucy

Providing nourishment to a dog and healing her physical ailments is one challenge. Offering proper training so a dog can happily thrive is quite another. Lucy definitely needed training. Fortunately, Catherine had experience in this department. Although it is rare for Great Danes to exhibit aggressive behavior, Lucy became quite contentious toward Maggie and Bodhi around food. Catherine knew that such tactics could be expected from any living being deprived of food and affection for such a long period of time. She worked with Lucy to rid her of any aggressive behavior that reared its head when food appeared.

There was also the matter of potty training. As one might imagine, any animal confined to a cage without any care is not going to be housebroken. So, yes, accidents happened in the house. Catherine was notified before she even saw the evidence. Maggie and Bodhi gave it away. The two magnificent Harlequin Danes huddled in the corner together with looks on their faces as if to say, "It's over there! We didn't do it! It wasn't us!" Lucy learned quickly from her tattle tale siblings how to use the doggie door to let herself out as she needed and pleased.

Lucy was really coming out of her shell. She followed Catherine from one room to another and started showering her with kisses. The wall she had up around people was now down. She showed a lot of gentle affection. She also started building relationships with her siblings. At first, Lucy displayed some unruly behavior as she tried to figure out where she belonged within the pack. Maggie and Bodhi both set her straight. Lucy accepted her place as the baby. It was not long until she started playing with and kissing them both. She especially loved Bodhi.

Lucy with Catherine

The day Catherine knew that Lucy was going to be okay was the day that she picked up a toy on her own and started to play. Catherine thought to herself, "She's really going make it!"

Looking back, it was quite an amazing feat. When she first came into Catherine's life, Lucy was checked out. She was ready to die. Now, she is a gentle soul with an exuberant, playful spirit! She spends time at the beach and the park. She enjoys going for walks and playing in the backyard where she loves to be squirted with the water sprayer. She's a chewer and thoroughly enjoys chomping on bones. But, most of all, she loves to cuddle. Every morning, she crawls into bed with Catherine to start her day with loving pets, warm hugs, and belly rubs.

Catherine and Lucy have a deep and genuine connection. Catherine describes it as telepathic. Lucy seems to pick up on Catherine's feelings and knows what she is thinking. In fact, they are often in the same mood. The pair share a gentle spirit and determined nature. All Lucy needed to flourish was someone to love and cherish her. That someone was and is Catherine. Lucy is a grateful girl. She knows she was saved.

Nearly four years after welcoming Lucy into the family, Catherine and her girls faced a tragic loss. Bodhi passed away Thanksgiving morning of 2013. Weeks after his passing, Lucy and Maggie could be found resting together and comforting each other in the spot where Bodhi used to lay.

TRIBUTE TO BODHI

by Catherine

My beloved Bodhi,

Thank you for the blessing of sharing your life with me.

Bodhi (photograph provided by Catherine)

For your incredibly sweet, kind, gentle, loving nature, and your fun-loving, silly sense of humor.

For always loving and protecting me; your brother, Nick; your sister, Maggie; and your adopted sister, Lucy.

I will be forever changed and am a better person because of you.

Until we meet again … run free and happy.

Missing you and loving you always,

Momma

12

PAYING LOVE AND KINDNESS FORWARD IS PAWSIBLE

On an evening in July 2012, a young woman was driving home from work along Memorial Drive in Atlanta, Georgia. She stopped at the light of a busy intersection and glanced at the familiar surroundings. Her eyes froze in disbelief when she spotted a painfully emaciated Red-Nosed American Pit Bull Terrier mix in the adjacent field. The woman slowly managed to pull over, and then approached the skin-and-bones animal with care. He had apparently been dumped. The forsaken dog's eyes were haunting as they stared at her from a sunken face plagued by starvation. His bones protruded sharply through his thin skin, which was marred by infected bug bites. When she reached him, she noticed that his tail had missing fur, likely from all those bug bites, and his paws were raw red. He was clearly in pain. He was desperate. Alone. Dying.

The woman brought the canine home that night. She named him Charlie. The next day, she took him to a veterinary medical center for care. He weighed a ghastly 34 pounds, which was about half of what he should weigh to be healthy. Charlie spent that night at the medical center. The woman picked him up the following day and brought him back to her home to spend his third night after being discovered. He wiggled his little butt with gratitude for her kindness, but had difficulty getting up the next morning. Desperate to save this sweet boy, the woman sent out a heartfelt plea for help on Facebook.

The post on Facebook was shared from one friend to another and another. One Atlanta woman who came across it immediately thought of her close friend, Melissa, Founder of Peace and Paws Rescue located in New Hampshire. She sent her an email containing the photograph. Upon opening it, Melissa's heart sank. The gut-wrenching photo of the pleading pup contained a caption with a simple question: Can you help him? There was just something about those eyes and that precious face. Melissa thought, "Yes, I have to help him!"

It was clear that Charlie's health was in a fragile state. There was no way that he was well enough to be transported via truck from Georgia to New Hampshire. He needed one-on-one attention and care to make the trip, so Melissa drove down to Atlanta in her own personal vehicle to pick him up and bring him north. On the first night of their two-day road trip, Melissa and Charlie stayed in a hotel. Charlie's devastating condition drew a lot of concerned stares. A wave of relief and gratitude washed away the fret on people's faces as Melissa explained her rescue mission to one person after another.

The next morning, Melissa and Charlie were on the road again. They stopped every five hours so Charlie could eat. It didn't take long for Charlie to realize that the woman by his side was a saint—a saint with food! Any time Melissa had to walk away from the car, he watched every move she made. Although he was still extremely weak, he ate and drank like a champ, and then fell fast asleep.

By now it was about two weeks since he had been rescued from that field in Atlanta. His destination was Concord, New Hampshire, where a kind foster family awaited his arrival. The couple took excellent care of two-year-old Charlie, including getting him to veterinarian visits. Most adult dogs from the south who are in such a detrimental state of health as Charlie test positive for heartworms. By some miracle, Charlie did not. This was so surprising that Melissa had him tested three times. Each test brought good news. No heartworms.

Charlie's foster family made sure to keep him well-nourished by giving him daily vitamins and feeding him small meals consisting of cooked chicken and rice, along with yogurt mixed into his kibble. It was important that he continue to eat every four to five hours in small amounts to slowly build up his digestive system and help him gain weight. To accomplish this, the couple arranged their work schedules so that one of them would go home every few hours to take Charlie out of his crate and feed him. Since he wasn't trained yet, there was no way he could be given full access to the house—or even a room in the house—when he was left alone.

At this point, Charlie was so grateful and attached to the humans that had entered his life and saved him that he became extremely nervous whenever he was left alone—as if he would be abandoned and left for dead again. Even though the couple tried their best to be with him as much as possible, he spent every moment that he was alone barking inside his crate. In fact, he was expending so much energy alerting the world to his worries that it counteracted his food intake, making it difficult for him to gain weight. The call for a new foster, who could spend nearly all hours of the day with him, went out.

In the meantime, Gale, a woman living in another town in New Hampshire, was mesmerized as she watched a video of a gentle and frail, yet determined, Charlie posted on Facebook. It was created by the woman who found him in the field in Atlanta. Charlie was standing outside. He walked toward his rescuer, laid his head on her lap, and then looked up at her and into the camera. He was so skinny that his body could not be seen behind his head.

Charlie's longing eyes pierced Gale's heart. Haunting. Vacant. Desperate. She had seen those eyes before. Not long ago, they had stared back at her in the mirror. Two years earlier, Gale's mother passed away. Shortly following this heartbreaking loss, a violent, brutal attack shattered Gale to her very core. Someone that she and her 9-year old American Bulldog, Olivia, both knew and trusted, broke into their home. With forceful and intentional will, he brutally violated Gale, as Olivia bore witness to it all.

The terrifying event left Olivia shaken. She was distressed by every little noise she heard. As for Gale, she coped by disconnecting from everyone. She withdrew from life and found herself at the bottom of a deep, dark pit—struggling with all her might to climb out. With time and care, she healed. With support from family and friends, she reached higher ground. Now, she was looking down into that pit and saw Charlie fighting for his life just as she had. She heard him calling to her. She reached out to him. She was there with open arms—ready and waiting for the opportunity to save him.

On July 28, 2012, Gale and Olivia went to meet Charlie. The dogs had a great introduction outside—sniffing each other's rear ends as doggies do. Tails were wagging, so they took the visit inside to tighter quarters. Gale was grinning from ear to ear. Charlie warmed her heart. The next day, she received a phone call that changed her life forever. "Hi, Gale! It's Melissa from Peace and Paws. Congratulations! You are the chosen one to foster and adopt Charlie."

Pure elation filled her soul. "Really? I'm so excited! Thank you so much."

Charlie arrived at his forever home with Gale on July 31, 2012. She was just two weeks away from retirement and had a bundle of vacation time built up. With Charlie's separation anxiety issues, she wanted to be home as much as possible. She made arrangements with her boss to work half days for the last couple of weeks before retirement. Charlie would only have to be left in his crate without her around for four hours a day—and only for a couple of weeks.

With Charlie now up to 48 pounds, Gale continued the same feeding regime as his previous fosters. She was a bit concerned that he did not drink water. Perhaps when he was trying to survive on his own in that field, he was drinking contaminated water that made him sick? It was a guess on Gale's part. Nonetheless, she had to be sneaky and mix yogurt with water so he would stay hydrated. Each day she put in less and less yogurt, until finally he drank plain water. On that thrilling day, Gale jumped for joy and lavished her boy with a great big a hug.

Shortly after his arrival, Charlie gave Gale a bit of a scare when blood started appearing in his stool. Thankfully, this was short-lived. Drawing on the help and expertise of Melissa at Peace and Paws Rescue, they determined that his intestine was aggravated by the transition from soft chicken to hard kibble. Even an extremely slow transition, as this was, can cause internal irritation. Within a couple of days, he was just fine.

Although Charlie was on his way to being nutritionally sound, he was still weak. He had no muscle tone. To make him strong, Gale started taking Charlie to physical therapy about once a week for two months to do hydrotherapy. Charlie walked on a treadmill partially submerged under water. The water served as resistance to help him build and tone his muscles.

At first, Charlie was scared to get on the treadmill. Gale had to lure him with treats. With each visit, he became a little more comfortable and it took less work to coax him onto the machine. By Charlie's last visit, he was a pro and hopped right on to do his thing.

In conjunction with the hydrotherapy, Gale took Charlie on short walks a few times a day. To help him build his back leg strength, the therapist gave Gale exercises for Charlie to perform on his walks. After walking a few feet, Gale would make Charlie sit, and then get up to walk a few more feet; sit and get up again. Repeat, repeat, and repeat.

Another transition that took time was allowing Charlie to eat in the same room with his new sister. Initially, Gale put Charlie in his crate to eat, and then fed Olivia in the kitchen. He was a dog gone wild at the sight of food. Who could blame him?

Each week, Charlie gained more control over his excitement at the sight and smell of food at feeding time. First, eating out of the crate, but in a different room than Olivia. As a next step, he was allowed in the kitchen, while Gale prepared his meal. It was a lot of work teaching him to be calm when food was present. Gale was consistent and patient with him until he reached the point where he could eat side-by-side with Olivia.

Obedience school came next. Basic training at American K9 Country helped Charlie gain confidence and tightened the already strong bond between him and Gale. He earned a ribbon and certificate, and then went on to do the same with AKC's Canine Good Citizen® training. It did wonders for Charlie. He was able to sit for three minutes with Gale out of the room. Separation anxiety? Be gone! A huge achievement and proud moment, indeed.

On September 11, 2012, Charlie's adoption was complete, making him an official member of Gale's family. As summer turned to fall and fall turned to winter, this southern boy morphed into a northern boy with great ease. Charlie greeted the mega amounts of snow that Jack Frost delivered with great exuberance, jumping in and running through the white stuff with Olivia. He spent his first Christmas hanging out around the Christmas tree singing—er, howling—carols to the sister he quickly grew to adore. Olivia adored him right back. Noises no longer frightened her as they did before Charlie came into her world. She became calmer with her brother around.

Charlie's personality transformed from worrywart to chillaxed dude. There was a point in time when he would not leave Gale's side. He hovered next to the shower anxiously awaiting Gale's exit. He would also intersect Gale's path to the front door and bark when she needed to leave the house. Now, he just hangs out in the bedroom or living room when Gale gets ready for the day. He is secure in knowing she will return soon anytime she heads out the door.

Charlie fell in love with his mom, sister and the rest of the family, including Gale's six young grandchildren. At a healthy weight of 72 pounds, he no longer lacked for love, hugs or attention, and showed immense gratitude for his good fortune. Every night when Gale took Charlie and Olivia out to go to the bathroom before bedtime, Charlie looked up to admire the moon and the stars. Gale told Melissa about this awesome sight that always made her smile, "You know, Melissa, most dogs look out and about, but Charlie always looks upward."

Melissa's heart filled with happiness at this match made in heaven, "That is Charlie thanking his lucky stars that he found you, Gale."

With a twinkle in her eye, Gale smiled brightly, "I rescued him, but he rescued me, too. We are meant to be. It was written in the stars."

Over the course of more than two years, the bonds between Gale, Charlie, and Olivia grew. The dogs shared countless adventures with Gale, and enjoyed cuddling and playing with each other. As each precious moment passed, time passed, too. Olivia grew older and her health declined. The deep love and gratitude Charlie felt for Olivia was captured in their last photograph together as he gave his sweet sister a kiss and cuddle goodbye. After a long, beautiful life, Olivia passed away peacefully.

A heartbroken Gale planted a tree in Olivia's memory and surrounded it with rocks. Her grandchildren, family, and friends helped Gale create a lovely memorial to Olivia by writing sweet messages and drawing heartfelt pictures with colorful markers on the rocks. The rock garden proudly displays Olivia's collar and tags, and was made complete with a gift of chimes that sing the voice of Olivia when the wind stirs.

Nearly six months after Olivia's passing, Gale's heart beckoned her to save another life. She turned to Peace and Paws Dog Rescue again. They recently saved a small, reddish-brown American Pit Bull Terrier mix. Daisy had been dumped at a shelter in Alabama. Her submissive and fearful behavior was so extreme that she crawled on her belly every time she entered or exited her kennel. When Melissa of Peace and Paws contacted the shelter to inquire about the pretty Pittie, she was told, "That dog is near the top of the euthanize list because of her skittish, submissive behavior. She won't be long for this world." Melissa knew she had to immediately arrange transport to get Daisy out to save her life, and she did.

At just two years old, Daisy had already had a litter of puppies. Her face, head, body, and legs were marred by scars with an unknown history, and she was mysteriously missing one of her canine teeth. A later checkup at the vet's office also revealed that her teeth were intentionally ground down by someone. They were short and smooth. All of these disfigurements were strong evidence that Daisy was once cruelly used by humans as a bait dog for their game fighting dogs.

Gale had a couple of visits with the little Pittie and easily fell in love with her docile demeanor. After Peace and Paws helped Daisy recover from the kennel cough she caught in the shelter, Charlie had the pleasure of meeting her, too. It was a successful match! Gale and Charlie happily welcomed Daisy into their family. Daisy was quick to display her affection, admiration and gratitude to both Gale and Charlie. She constantly had to be near one of them—preferably both of them. She genuinely loved people and greeted all her new human friends with the wiggliest of wiggle butts.

Along with physical scars, Gale quickly became witness to the deep emotional scars this timid girl bared. Loud banging noises put Daisy in fright and flight mode. If it weren't for Gale taking strong hold of her leash, Daisy would run scared every time she heard the slam of a car door, or even the thwacking open and close of the squeaky mailbox.

One morning, Daisy accidentally knocked over the recycle bin. The noise frightened her, but even more, she cowered in terror and ran to hide in a corner. Sadness emerged as Gale witnessed Daisy's deep-seated fear. It was clear she thought she was in trouble. It was clear she thought she would be beaten.

Gale tenderly sat on the floor next to an uneasy Daisy to offer her love and comfort with gentle pets and a quiet, easy voice, "Miss Daisy, whatever happened to you before; however badly you were treated; you will never have to endure such cruelty ever again. You are safe here. You are safe." Charlie calmly made his way over to offer his new sister a loving nuzzle.

Daisy is learning the meanings of love and kindness. Gale and Charlie are showing her. Just as both of them were helped out of darkness, they are helping Daisy out of darkness. That's what rescue is all about—paying love and kindness forward.

13

TAKING A STAND FOR ANIMALS IS PAWSIBLE

In spring of 2010, a Coon Hound puppy—just 5 weeks old—was picked up as a stray and brought to Robeson County Animal Shelter in North Carolina. There were no signs of her momma or siblings. She was all alone.

Coon Hounds are bred for hunting dogs in North Carolina. A popular sport, hunting is taken quite seriously in these parts. According to local residents, it is common practice for hunters to keep their hunting dogs in a small pen without socializing them. In an effort to make them more aggressive on the hunt, they also starve their dogs—not enough to make them malnourished, but enough to make them ravaged by hunger and extremely eager for prey. If a dog is not performing up to snuff, he or she is tossed out like a broken tool. Some are driven to, and then deserted in the woods. Others are ditched in neighborhoods or dumped in high kill shelters, like Robeson County Animal Shelter.

A young Coon Hound arrived at this shelter when it was under public fire for inhumane practices. To say their treatment of animals was cruel is an understatement. It's hard to say what happened to the puppy's family, but her fate would be revealed over the next couple of weeks.

WARNING! THE FOLLOWING CONTAINS GRAPHIC DESCRIPTIONS OF THE TORTUROUS TREATMENT OF INNOCENT ANIMALS.

The shelter's savage practices can be traced back to at least 2001 when video was taken showing a two-man team ruthlessly killing dogs one after another with absolutely no sedation used at all. In the video, the first man is seen dragging animals one by one into a room by their necks with a catch pole. As if knowing their fate, dog after dog writhed desperately in an effort to escape the forceful choke hold. The second man in this methodical act of evil stabbed each frightened soul with a heart stick*. One helpless being after another is thrown in a pile in the back of the shelter. Discarded like trash, each and every one died torturous, agonizing deaths—some more slowly than others.

*Heart sticking. *Known medically as intracardial injections, there is no sedation involved. Sodium pentobarbital is passed through the chest wall and layers of muscle into the heart with a needle and syringe, known as a heart stick. When an animal is fully conscious, their body is in constant motion, so it is extremely difficult for the person administering the injection to reach the ventricle chamber for an instant, painless death. More commonly, a lung is punctured, which causes fluid to fill the lungs and results in an excruciating death for the animal.*

These disgraceful euthanasia methods practiced at this shelter were brought to the limelight in winter 2010. A woman, who ran a rescue located in St. Paul, Minnesota, went on a road trip with her husband to the shelter in North Carolina with the intent to save as many dogs as they could fit in their trailer. After witnessing, firsthand, their abuse and unethical treatment toward the animals, she wrote an impassioned letter directly to the person in charge at Robeson County Health Department describing all she saw and heard.

One of the more disturbing scenes took place while she was tending to a frightfully thin dog that had recently given birth. The woman overheard a worker in the shelter rage, "Now, suffer on this you son of a bitch!" When she went to see what was going on, she saw two workers with a pole jabbing something. As documented in her letter, what followed were "the most horrific screams from an animal that I have ever heard in my whole life. The men sat over the dog and laughed as it screamed in pain for about two minutes."

The heart-wrenching letter drew a flurry of media attention. It resulted in a lawsuit filed against the shelter and a trial ensued.

During the trial, it was revealed that the shelter was putting down more than fifty animals a week. In addition to the heart sticking, shotgun casings were found in the shelter—evidence that they were actually shooting dogs. The shelter denied the accusation, claiming instead that there was a raccoon in the shelter that they shot and killed.

In addition to the direct animal torture, the kennels and animals inside them were neglected. There were dead kittens and puppies left in kennels for days with their living mommas and other siblings. The shelter staff rarely cleaned the kennels. Many animals were left with no food or water. Those who did have water had contaminated water—mold growing on the plastic bowls. Some bowls even had bowel movements inside. The dog beds were nothing more than a wooden pallet.

The kennels were aligned in such a way that there were grates in the middle of the floor for drainage. When the workers would actually clean the kennels they would throw bleach on floors and then spray it down while the dogs were still inside. Many dogs came out of the shelter with chemical burn marks on the pads of their feet and skin problems from getting sprayed with the bleach.

THE GRAPHIC DESCRIPTIONS OF TORTUROUS TREATMENT OF INNOCENT ANIMALS ARE OVER.

The trial resulted in a policy change. Robeson County Animal Shelter was ordered to end heart sticking and a press conference was held in front of the shelter to make the announcement. Camera crews were all around to report it.

On this same day, a couple who founded Helping Every Animal Live (H.E.A.L.), located in Jacksonville, North Carolina, were at the shelter delivering Kuranda beds. Michele and her husband, Carlos, raised $4000 to purchase these beds for the animals in the shelter.

Before entering the shelter, the pair made a pact, "We already have five dogs. We cannot get another one." Once inside, Michele went about placing the Kuranda beds in the kennels. She took her time in each kennel. They were filthy and many had no food or water. She cleaned and filled their bowls with water. Determined to keep the pact she made with her husband, Michele gave the dogs treats, but kept them at an arm's length away.

The couple arrived at the Coon Hound puppy's kennel. After placing a bed inside, Carlos headed back to the car to get more beds. Michele followed suit, but happened to glance back over her shoulder. She and the precious girl locked eyes, stopping her in her tracks. Then, something magical happened. A spark ignited and a deep connection instantly took hold. Michele walked back and knelt down outside the girl's kennel. Tears poured down her face.

With pleading eyes, the puppy spoke to Michele's warm heart, "My name's Charlie. Get me out of here, please."

Carlos returned from outside. He stopped and watched his lovely wife. With a gentle smile, he walked up to Michele. "We're taking her home, aren't we?"

"Yes."

Michele took a picture of Charlie's kennel card. At this shelter, they held dogs for 120 hours before making them eligible for adoption. Charlie's 120 hours would be up at 2:00 p.m. on a Saturday. The shelter closed at 1:00 p.m. on Saturdays and wasn't open on Sundays.

Michele asked the administrator of the shelter, "Would you let me come up Saturday to adopt her?"

The man was unyielding with his reply, "No. We need to follow the rules."

Michele pleaded, "The problem is that you kill on Mondays before you open the shelter and her time will have been up Monday before you open. I want to adopt her."

"Call Saturday right before we close to make sure that she's still here."

A red flag wildly rose and Michele's stomach dropped. Even though they were supposed to hold dogs that were knowingly going to be adopted or rescued on Mondays, the shelter had a documented history of killing those dogs. In fact, Michele knew about a reported instance in which a woman stood outside the shelter and could actually hear the killing as it happened. It was later discovered that it was one of the dogs that the woman was there to get that they killed. Michele did not want this happening to Charlie.

Desperate to save Charlie's life, Michele chose to comply with the administrator's instructions. "That's fine. I'll do that."

This particular shelter is a three hour drive for Michele—one way. The administrator knew that. He instructed, "Call on Monday, too, before you drive all that way because funny stuff happens here on the weekends. You'll want to make sure she's here."

Michele bit her tongue again for the sake and safety of Charlie. In an effort to stay on the man's good side, she put on a façade of jest, "Oh, I'm sure it's going to be just fine. You'll take good care of her."

For six long, agonizing days Michele had to wait for Charlie. Her stomach was in knots with worry because she was well aware of all the recorded abuse that went on at the shelter. She knew that Charlie's chances of survival were slim. She had to do all she could to increase those chances.

Although Michele was not legally involved in the lawsuit against the shelter, she had done a lot of investigative work and raised much money for abandoned and abused animals in the area. People involved in the case and associated with the shelter knew her. As she anxiously waited for Monday to arrive, Michele used social media to announce that she was going to adopt Charlie. She posted a photograph of the sweet girl so that everyone was aware—including those at the shelter—that she would be there first thing Monday to get her puppy. After six harrowing days, Michele and Carlos headed back to the shelter.

Arriving before it opened Monday morning, she banged on the office doors and the shelter doors to make it known that she was there and ready to adopt Charlie. Finally, the doors opened. Michele went straight to Charlie's kennel, but she was not there.

With a pounding, heavy heart she raced through the shelter searching for her.

There! There's Charlie! The shelter crew had moved her from her original kennel to another. Her surroundings were filthy and Charlie smelled. She had no bed. The Kuranda beds she and Carlos delivered just days earlier had been moved out of the kennels. Nobody knew who moved them or why.

The young pup was covered in fleas and a fews ticks. She was full of every type of internal parasite imaginable and extremely underweight. But, she was alive! And now she belonged to Michele and Carlos.

With every intention of getting her doctored up, and then adopting her out in six months, Michele and Carlos drove Charlie straight to their vet in Jacksonville, North Carolina. She got a thorough checkup. With attentive care over the next few weeks, Charlie's belly ridded itself of parasites and her skin cleared up after being diagnosed with a bacterial infection. Although she was severely underweight, it did not take Charlie long to beef up.

During the weeks of Charlie's recuperation to full health, many news stories came out about the trial and the shelter. The administrator was moved out. A fresh crew was brought in. The Kuranda beds that H.E.A.L. so generously donated to Robeson County Animal Shelter were placed back into the kennels and put to full use.

The hold policy at the shelter changed. Before the trial, they would hold dogs for five days, and then kill them without ever putting them up for adoption. After the trial, it was declared that dogs be held for five days, but must be made visible to the public after their first 72 hours in an attempt to get them adopted. Although they could still euthanize, the shelter switched to a much more humane method—intravenous injection. Most importantly, the abuse stopped. All these changes not only went into effect at this shelter, but all shelters statewide. They became state law.

As Michele watched several of the news clips that aired making the announcements, she caught glimpses of Charlie's precious puppy face on TV. With all those cameras around during her stay, Charlie caught a lot of eyes and became a local TV star. The thought did not escape Michele that Charlie's life very well may have been saved by the media—both news crews and Michele's social media postings.

Michele and Carlos reminisced about Charlie's rescue. Carlos asked, "Remember how you said the name Charlie just came to you?"

Michele nodded with a soft smile looking down at the sweet girl nuzzled in her lap.

"Did you know that Carlos is Spanish for Charlie? My grandmother is the only person who ever called me that."

Knowing how extremely close Carlos was to his grandmother, Michele's eyes welled up with happy tears and her smile grew wide.

"I think the day Charlie spoke to you in the kennel, Grandma was trying to tell us that we need to bring her home."

So, she was home. Six months came and went. Charlie had Michele's heart and wasn't going anywhere.

Today, Charlie starts each day with a run through the yard with her sister, Phoebe. Michele is never surprised when Charlie brings a pine cone inside the house to shred—an amusement she picked up from her beloved, older brother, Einstein. What once was a hobby the two happily shared is now an homage that Charlie pays to Einstein's memory. When she isn't romping and roaming through the yard or shredding pine cones in the house, Charlie can be found sleeping sweetly and soundly, preferably in Carols and Michele's bed.

14

DEDICATING YOUR LIFE TO SERVING ANIMALS AND YOUR COMMUNITY IS PAWSIBLE

In 2006, Kym and Phil were experiencing a lot of changes in their lives. Having been married for a small handful of years, they purchased a new home and were preparing for an empty nest. Kym had two children from a previous marriage. Her daughter was already moved out, and her son was ready to wrap up junior high school and enter the world of senior high.

On top of all this change, Kym was fighting an inner battle. A work-related back injury forced her to take medical leave from work for nine long months. During this time, Kym was also diagnosed with fibromyalgia. The two excruciating physical ailments joined forces to infringe upon Kym's emotional well-being. Life felt dull, dark, and painful.

To keep the intense physical pain under control, Kym's doctor prescribed medication. Unfortunately, it amplified her depression. The daily despair she felt was so heavy that getting out of bed was difficult. In fact, some days she couldn't. Even the brightest, sunniest of days were dark. Living life? Well, Kym wasn't doing it.

In an effort to focus on something outside herself and push away the melancholy, Kym approached her husband with an idea, "Phil, sweetie, we've talked about it before, and I think the time is finally right. What do you think about getting a dog?"

Phil's eyes lit up. "I think that's a great idea!"

The pair went to spcaLA in Long Beach, California, where Kym became completely enamored with a Doberman Pinscher. Murphy slipped right up to the kennel gate and looked up at her with batting eyelashes pleading for gentle pets and love. He knew how to work it! Murphy's strong kennel presence was irresistible.

With fingers and toes crossed, Phil and Kym exchanged excited, yet nervous, looks as they submitted their adoption application.

"Are you ready for this?" Phil asked.

"I think so." Kym wanted to be completely enthusiastic, but part of her wondered whether their application would be approved. There was no reason it wouldn't be, but she had her heart set on Murphy. She could not face the disappointment of not being able to adopt him.

Later that day, the couple received a call, "Congratulations! You have a new family member."

In a state of shock, Kym hung up the phone and walked over to her hubby. "Looks like we're doing this!"

Kym and Phil welcomed Murphy into their home with open arms. This hyperactive Dobie had been found on the streets of Long Beach. He went through the city's shelter system—ultimately, ending up at spcaLA. Now, he had a loving, forever home with Kym and Phil.

It didn't take the couple long to realize Murphy was a bit neurotic. Phil opened the door to let him outside for a potty break. Observing that the grass was wet, Murphy put himself in reverse, refusing to walk on the misted greens. He looked up at Phil, turned his head to look out at the wet grass, looked up at Phil again, and then darted back into the house. Thoroughly amused by this crazy, funny boy's obsessive compulsions, Kym giggled.

On another occasion, during backyard play time, Murphy accidently stepped in poop. Limping and gimping on three legs as if injured, he turned to Kym in a ploy for assistance. With a furrowed brow, Murphy batted his eyelashes at her as if to say, "Look. Look! Would you just look at my paw? A little help, please?"

His zealous ways were more than a distraction to Kym—they were seeds of hope and renewal. Phil was delighted to see his wife's face light up again. As she watched Murphy, Phil watched her. Although Kym was still struggling, Phil saw glimpses of sparkling light making a comeback into Kym's eyes. Three months after adopting him, Kym approached Phil, "Honey, Murphy has so much energy. I think a playmate would do him good. What do you think?"

Phil looked at his wife with a growing smile, "What kind of dog are you thinking?"

"A Lab. A Black Lab would be a good match."

The couple found Chloe at Southeast Area Animal Control Authority (SEAACA) in Downey, California. Kym spotted the emaciated Black Labrador Retriever the minute she was brought into the kennels. Chloe was a stray and hadn't even been inside the shelter walls long enough to have a kennel card. Kym watched as the sweet girl was put in a kennel with three very scared bully breed mixes. One of them was a female in heat. The dynamic made Chloe nervous. Worry and self-doubt were written all over her frail face.

Kym approached one of the employees, "I would like to adopt the Black Lab that was just brought in."

"We need to hold her for ten days, but I can put you at the top of the list if anybody else wants to adopt her."

Murphy jumping for joy as Chloe (front right) and soon-to-be adopted Bailey (front left) look on

No one ever did. Ten days later, Murphy had a new sister.

At 10 months old, skeletal Chloe weighed a mere 35 pounds when Kym and Phil brought her home. She needed to more than double her weight to reach a healthy 80 pounds for her frame. She was so starved that her fur was molting off, and her high anxiety level was adding to the fur loss. Just laying in her crate, fur was dropping off her skin.

"C'mon, sweetie. Let's get you a bath." As Kym gently pet her to make her feel at ease, Chloe's fur fell off in handfuls. It took seven baths to get the fur loss under control.

Things were touch and go for awhile in her new home. Kym and Phil were not sure Chloe was going to make it. In addition to her starved body, she also had mange and an extreme case of kennel cough. Very much wrecked and overwhelmed with worry, Chloe would not come out of her crate. Observing her, Kym thought back. Just a few months ago, *she* was having trouble getting out of bed. Chloe gave Kym the magical gift of purpose.

As Kym and Phil tended to Chloe's physical health, Murphy tended to her emotional health. He was lively, yet gentle and kind. Just as Murphy was to Kym, he was also to Chloe—the perfect medicine for her soul.

"I've got an idea," Kym told her husband.

The couple moved the dogs' crates so that Chloe and Murphy faced each other. They also left the doors open. Although Chloe remained inside her hiding place, the sight of Murphy provided her comfort as a baby blanket does for a toddler. His presence wiped the angst away from her face. She was slow to warm, but Murphy was ever so patient with her. He knew exactly how to make her feel at ease, which was no easy feat considering Chloe was afraid of her own shadow.

With his outgoing charm, Murphy tried to engage Chloe. He nuzzled with her. Poked at her. He would stick his butt in the air and wiggle his tail, while his face and paws were on the floor in front of Chloe coaxing her with a happy grin to come out and play. His attempts went unreciprocated, but he persisted. Quietly amused, she never took her eyes off him. Before Chloe could reach the point of annoyance, Murphy cuddled with her.

After a couple of weeks, Murphy's steadfast coaxing paid off. Chloe quietly poked her head out from her safe haven. Moving slowly and carefully toward Murphy, her healing body emerged from hiding. Kym's face lit up.

She whispered and nudged her husband with excitement and gratitude, "Phil, look!"

Murphy welcomed Chloe's approach with smiles, licks, and a wagging tail. Kym and Phil joined in the love fest offering Chloe and Murphy plenty of pets and hugs, and getting a lot of wet kisses in return.

Each day Chloe grew stronger, healthier, and more confident. She was so bonded to Murphy that she would not leave the front part of the house without him. Neither Kym nor Phil could take her on a walk without her buddy. If Murphy wasn't going, she wasn't going. She would stop, plop down, and lay on the ground until Murphy showed his happy face. This lasted for about a year.

Since adopting Murphy, then Chloe, the heavy weight of depression Kym carried got lighter with each passing day. Her heart was filled with gratitude for these two canines. She knew they saved her life. Cuddling with them on the couch one evening, Kym picked up the DVD remote and pressed Play to watch the movie, *Sweet November*, starring Charlize Theron and Keanu Reeves. She was suddenly transfixed by a scene at the beach. Charlize Theron's character walked five white Standard Poodles to the beach and let them off their leashes to run footloose and fancy-free along the shore. As Kym watched the dogs play with complete abandonment—running, jumping, rolling in the sand—she thought, "If dogs can be that happy and not care about anything else around them, why can't I?" Suddenly, she felt so light, as if she could fly. She decided then and there, it was time to live. Really, truly live!

A year after welcoming their first dog into the family, Kym and Phil happened to be in the neighborhood and decided to pop into SEAACA. They weren't looking for a third dog, but a black ball of matted fur got Phil as excited as a kid at Christmastime. The four month old puppy clearly had a severe case of mange. Along with patches of missing fur, the mange left the pup completely bald around his eyes.

"He looks like a Newfoundland. Such cool dogs!"

"He might be part Newf, sweetie, but his intake card claims he's a Chow mix."

"Really? He looks more like a Newfie to me. I've always wanted one, Kymmie! My brothers had them when I was growing up, and I just always wanted one."

Kym knew what was coming. Looking at the matted ball of black out of the corner of her eye and wearing a curious "should-I-give-in?" smirk, she continued listening to her husband's reasoning and request.

"The other two dogs are getting along just fine. This little guy, well, he's a puppy so we can raise him and train him. No one else is going to want him because of the mange. He looks like a ratty ball of fur. I think we should bring him home."

Not totally convinced, but wanting her husband to be happy, Kym replied, "Okay, honey."

After waiting several days for him to be neutered, they eagerly returned to SEAACA to pick up the dog they concluded was a Newfie, and named him Guinness. As Kym pet him on the ride home, she discovered a thin cat collar beneath all the matted fur. "Phil, if this little collar was on him any longer, it would have embedded itself into his skin. I can't believe they didn't find it and remove it when he was neutered. He wouldn't have received much attention at the shelter at all. Good thing you found him!"

With much love and tender care from Kym and Phil, Guinness was a happy, healthy canine within three months. As he grew, they realized he wasn't likely a Newfoundland mix after all.

Guinness

"Kymmie, the more Guinness grows, the less he looks like a Newfie. What do you think he's mixed with?"

"I think he looks a lot like a Flat-Coated Retriever."

For a few years, Kym and Phil agreed that Guinness was likely a Flat-Coated Retriever, but curiosity eventually got the better of them. They had his DNA tested.

"Phil, you're never going to believe the results of Guinness's DNA test."

"They came in? Tell me!"

"He is Alaskan Malamute, Golden Retriever, AND … are you ready for it?"

"Those two are kind of surprising, but make sense. What else? I'm dying!"

"American Staffordshire Terrier!"

"What? Really? Never would have guessed he's part Pit Bull. That's so cool."

"He's so wonderful. It's terrifying to think that in some cities and states he could be confiscated and euthanized just for his bloodline. Just because he's part Pit Bull."

"I don't know what I would do. Guinness is my boy! Breed discrimination needs to stop. It really does."

"The best dogs are rescued dogs. Breed doesn't really matter. Temperament does. Blending personalities and energies matters. "

"Thanks to you, I think our pack is really well-balanced and blended. You've got a keen instinct for matching dogs, Kymmie." Phil kissed her cheek.

"Thank you, sweetie."

"What else are you thinking? You have that deep thoughts look."

"Remember when we first saw Guinness at the shelter? His card said he was a Chow. I was just thinking about how much guesswork takes place at shelters every day, and how it can potentially affect the lives of shelter animals and their chances of adoption."

"That's true. If I was dead set on him being a Newfoundland or concerned about him being a Chow, like the shelter thought, we may not have adopted him."

"Exactly."

"It was more important to me to save a good puppy who had slim chances of getting adopted. I saw the potential he had to be a great dog. And, that's exactly what we got."

When Guinness was about six months old, Kym pointed out, "Honey, we need a partner for Guinness. He's such a silly, goofy puppy. He needs a mature partner to balance that."

"Maybe a German Shepherd?"

"Yeah. That could be a good match. I'll see what I can find online at the shelters."

Kym went back to SEAACA to meet a German Shepherd she picked out online at Petfinder.com. As much as Kym wanted to save the female dog, her energy level was too high to fit in with their pack. A little disappointed, Kym turned around to find a delightful surprise. Bailey was a ten month old Australian Shepherd. Kym said hello to her, and then continued walking through the kennels. As she did, the girl watched her intently.

Bailey

Kym approached a member of the shelter staff, "I'd like to meet that Aussie. Can I have a few minutes with her?"

"Absolutely. She's one of our True Blue Friends."

"What's that?"

"She's an exceptional dog and one of the staff favorites. Unfortunately, this is her third time back at the shelter. None of us want to see her euthanized because she's so awesome. It's not her fault she keeps ending up back here. She really deserves a wonderful home."

"What's her story?"

"She was born on the streets and ended up here at SEAACA for the first few months of her life. I think at one point she was mistaken for a Rottweiler mix because of her coloring. The family that adopted her wanted her to guard the backyard. Well, that was big mistake. What they didn't realize is that they were leaving a super bright, energetic herding dog alone in their yard with nothing to do. So, of course, she's going to find ways to entertain herself. That family wasn't too happy that she pulled plants and trees out of the ground. They returned her saying, 'She's tearing up the yard.' They didn't want her."

"She is so well-balanced!" Kym couldn't stop admiring this beauty who captivated her with her attentive eyes, and donned a soft, fluffy coat.

"Yeah, she's so sweet, too."

The SEAACA employee added, "She has no aggression issues whatsoever. She's very loving and attentive, and listens well. Aside from the time she was mistaken for a Rottie, I don't know how she ended up here three times. She's such a cool dog!"

Kym knew Bailey would blend in perfectly with their pack. This mature, astute herding dog had a need to be in control, which was an excellent match for young, free-spirited Guinness. She would also mingle well with Murphy's hyper personality and Chloe's insecurities.

With a pack of four rescued dogs, Kym found her passion. She had a natural knack for assessing temperaments and blending personalities to create well-balanced packs. Although Kym made it look easy, it can be challenging introducing and integrating dogs. It is not a task to be taken lightly. She and Phil were also strong, yet loving pack leaders.

Kym started volunteering as a dog handler for Best Friends Animal Society, Los Angeles. On her third day of volunteering and at her first public event, one of the Best Friends event leaders approached Kym, "Would you please walk Liberty around the event today? We'd really love to see her get adopted."

Liberty was a beautiful white Pit Bull speckled with silver. She was owned by a guy in South Los Angeles, along with thirteen other dogs. The man was breeding illegally and selling the dogs off for $300 to $800 each. Some were believed to have been sold for dog fighting. Liberty spent the first five to six years of her life as a breeding dog, most likely because of her unique silver freckled coloring.

The guy was finally caught and went to jail for his crimes. His case took nearly ten months to go through the system. During that time, the City of Los Angeles held on to Liberty at the North Valley Shelter as an evidence dog. Originally named Tina by the shelter staff, she was considered property (evidence) in a legal case and had to be "stored." That meant no human contact, no play time, no interaction with other dogs. Essentially, Liberty was in jail for a crime she did not commit. She was placed in an outside kennel and cubby where she was exposed to the chill of winter and extreme heat of summer.

The people at the shelter knew exactly how sweet Liberty was. From time to time, they broke the rules a bit by giving her a little extra outdoor time. Even so, she spent ten months in the LA shelter system confined inside a narrow 3' x 8' kennel with a back area that was a mere 3' x 3'. Made of concrete, it did not bode well for comfort. Since the kennels were sprayed down often, finding a dry area to lay down was difficult.

When the case was settled, all of the dogs being held as evidence for it were signed over to the city. All but one of Liberty's counter parts were adopted or pulled by local rescues. She wasn't either.

Over the Fourth of July, Best Friends hosted an adoption event. Along with Liberty, the City of Los Angeles brought in some other dogs that were under their ownership in an effort to get them all adopted. Those who were not adopted at the event were scheduled to go back to LA Animal Services and potentially be euthanized, including Liberty.

Kym was more than happy to spend the day with Liberty and show her off at the event. "Come on, girl. Let's get you adopted!"

Walking around the event, Liberty was all smiles. It was as if every person and dog she encountered was a dose of a happy pill. A walk. Interaction with others. So simple. So greatly appreciated.

When Kym took her lunch break, she put Liberty in her kennel. She returned to quite a sight. Liberty showed the stress of being confined. She was spinning round and round her kennel. Poop flew all around the inside. Her nails were cut open and her quicks were showing. As a result, there was blood smeared inside the kennel, too. Ten months of confinement had taken a toll on her. Liberty was a mess. As soon as Kym took her out of that kennel, she was fine. Covered in poop and blood, but fine.

Best Friends approached Kym, "You are a wonderful dog handler. Since you have a pack of your own, would you be interested in adopting Liberty? Or, even fostering her? You could take her overnight and evaluate how she does with your dogs."

Kym was intrigued by the idea. "Hmmm. My husband would enjoy it as much as me. Yes! We'll do it."

Kym took Liberty to her home to spend the night. Knowing how balanced her pack was and how much Liberty loved other dogs, Kym decided to just walk straight into the house with her. It worked. No pre-introductions were needed. Liberty fit right in.

Caution! Kym is an experienced dog trainer with a keen talent for matching and integrating canines. It is recommended to introduce dogs in neutral territory. Integrating animals can be a difficult, yet rewarding transition. Consult with a dog trainer for questions or concerns.

"Phil, sweetie, this is the momma I was telling you about." It was love at first sight for "Momma" and Phil!

Kneeling down to give her pets, Phil was smothered with sweet Liberty kisses. "Oh, Momma! You need a bath!"

After getting her cleaned up, Kym set out her crate. "As long as she has visuals of the other dogs, I don't think she'll go kennel crazy."

"Let me help you, Kymmie. Here next to Murphy and Chloe's crates is good."

Liberty, who quickly became known to Kym and Phil as Momma, slept peacefully and soundly.

Kym brought her back to the multi-day adoption event. It was like a repeat of the previous day. She was completely happy and content walking around and meeting people, but as soon as she was put into the kennel, she started spinning. No one showed any interest in Momma. Kym brought her home. For the next several months Kym and Phil brought her to adoption event after adoption event in hopes of finding a wonderful home for her. They both felt badly for this sweet girl.

"How long has Momma been staying with us, Kym?"

"I think it's been nine months now. Do you believe it? She's so wonderful! I wish everyone else saw what we see."

"What do you think about pulling the plug on this? We've been taking her here and there to every adoption event possible. I think we should just adopt her."

"She is really happy here. I just think the average person isn't up for taking in an eight-year-old Pit Bull that acts like a puppy."

Even though her personality was playful and rambunctious, her hard life showed in her body: broken teeth, sore gums, a hernia—she had litter after litter for many years. Add to that the stigma attached to Pit Bulls. Her chances of getting adopted were pretty slim.

Delaney

"Kymmie, I think Momma is already home. And, I also think I'd like to call her Delaney."

"Momma Delaney. I like it."

Six months after officially adopting Delaney, Kym came across a video of a nine-month-old black and tan Bernese Mountain Dog/Rottweiler mix posted online by Baldwin Park Animal Shelter. In the video, a dog handler is holding Dublin close, like a child cuddles a teddy bear. As she pet him, he held out his oversized puppy paw to hold her hand, and then kissed her face. Clearly affectionate, Dublin was also gentle, well-socialized, and exceptionally well-behaved. Kym's heart melted.

She and Phil happened to be volunteering at the Christmas Eve adoption event at Baldwin Park shelter. "Oh, Phil! I'm so excited to meet Dublin. I'm sure he will be there."

Much to their surprise and disappointment, Dublin wasn't there. He had been transferred the day before to Agoura Hills Animal Shelter.

The couple spent several hours loving on the homeless animals at Baldwin Park shelter. Kym adored them all, but her heart continued to pull her toward Dublin.

"I just love those black and tans, Phil! Do you mind driving to Agoura Hills? I keep replaying the video of him in my head. He's such a cuddly, crawl-in-your-lap kind of dog."

After the adoption event, Phil and Kym drove 90 minutes to Agoura Hills to meet Dublin. Meeting him confirmed what Kym thought. She couldn't get enough of him.

"He's pretty awesome, Kymmie. The only possible hurdle now is Guinness."

"Yes, he can be a little sassy. We should come back with him and introduce them. Just to be sure."

The next day, they loaded Guinness into the car and drove, yet again, one-and-a-half hours for a meet and greet between Guinness and Dublin. The puppy was not only adorable, but smart. He offered no challenge to Guinness and just let him be the alpha dog. After giving his humans a quick glance of approval, Guinness turned his attention back to Dublin and started to play.

Since it was the holidays, Kym and Phil had to wait to bring Dublin home until after the new year when he could be neutered.

"It's hard to wait, Phil. He definitely needs to be neutered, but it's still hard to wait!"

"No kidding. Hey, did you find out his back story? Why is he in the shelter?"

"He was an owner surrender. I can't believe anyone could give him up."

"Good thing you found him, Kymmie. Now he has a forever family," He smiled at his wife.

After patiently waiting out the holidays and spending ten days in Baldwin Park shelter, then fifteen more days in Agoura Hills shelter, Dublin caught kennel cough. He couldn't be neutered in such an ill state.

Dublin

The shelter staff tried to get him healthy. In the end, Kym and Phil placed a deposit for his neuter surgery so they could bring him home and nurse him back to health. They brought him back at a later date to get neutered.

Kym and Phil were so thrilled to get Dublin out of the shelter and bring him home that it didn't faze them at all when he experienced some motion sickness during the long ride home and threw up in the car.

Once in his new home, Dublin settled in with the rest of the pack and bonded with Momma Delaney quickly. It soon became apparent that, like Murphy, Dublin was neurotic. However, he entertained himself with his obsessions. Phil came home from work one day to a sight that swept a wide smile across his face and made his heart sing. His wife was peering out a window to the backyard and laughing out loud. That twinkle in her eyes that he knew and loved was not only back, but it was brighter than he'd ever seen.

"What's so funny?"

"That goofy Dublin is at it again. He has been running back and forth chasing shadows for hours!"

Phil walked up behind her, wrapped his arms around her, and rested his chin on her shoulder as he joined her to watch Dublin's comedy act. "He really is special, isn't he?"

Delaney and Guinness

Laughing out loud, Kym agreed, then took a serious tone, "We have quite a pack. I don't know where I would be without them. They saved me."

Phil hugged his wife tighter and kissed her gently on the cheek.

Delaney and Bailey (front, left to right); Dublin and Chloe (back, left to right)

Delaney, Chloe, Murphy, Dublin (left to right)

When Kym and Phil aren't being highly entertained by their canine six pack, they are often volunteering for Best Friends. Kym's children volunteer, too. For their summer vacation, Kym and Phil traveled to Kanub, Utah, with Delaney and Dublin to volunteer at The Sanctuary of Best Friends Animal Society.

Kym was crowned Mrs. Long Beach 2013 and Mrs. Southern California Cities 2014. During her reigns, she often brought one of her dogs to events she attended. Wearing her sash and crown in the company of one of her beloved adopted canines provided a perfect opportunity for her to talk about rescue, local shelters, and adoption, along with the importance of spay/neuter and behavioral issues. Kym isn't the only pageant winner in the family. In 2012, Delaney was runner-up in a local Pit Bull beauty pageant. In 2014, she placed first!

Kym and Phil with their six pack – from left to right:
Bailey, Dublin, Murphy, Delaney, Guinness and Chloe

The dogs that Kym and Phil adopted together ignited a passion. Kym is a dedicated animal advocate directly involved in many rescue events in Southern California. She continues volunteering for Best Friends and works in the animal care industry. Phil serves and protects the community as a long-time, dedicated police officer.

Kym and Phil are not only living life, they are making a positive difference in the lives of animals and their community.

15

RECEIVING AN UNEXPECTED GIFT IS PAWSIBLE

"When I look into the eyes of an animal, I do not see an animal. I see a living being. I see a friend. I feel a soul." –Anthony Douglas Williams.

Sugar was a beautiful seven year old Border Collie mix that had been with her family since she was six weeks old. She was not spayed and had never been vetted or given any preventatives. Sugar was not allowed in the house. Her home was the backyard. One day, a stray, unneutered dog came traipsing into her backyard, had his fun, and then trotted off. The result was a surprise litter of puppies.

The family was able to find homes for all of the puppies with the exception of one. Bella was born without eyes and nobody wanted her. When she was about 10 months old, the family decided to move from Georgia to Louisiana. They also decided they could not bring Sugar or Bella with them and posted an ad on Craig's List, offering the mother-daughter duo "free to a good home."

Alarmed and concerned for the safety of these dogs offered to anyone free of charge, a woman named Kendra reached out to the family:

"Hi there! I'm writing about your ad and have a wonderful suggestion to help make sure your dogs go to a great home. I have a lot of friends involved in the dog rescue community. Would you mind if I reached out to them to see if any can help you find them a great home?"

She received a reply:

"That would be fine. If we don't find a home for them by moving day, we will need to take both to the shelter."

One of the rescues that Kendra reached out to was Toni Diamond Rescue. Without hesitation, Toni stepped up to the plate. She contacted the owner. "With your permission, I am more than happy to take your dogs in. I will get them transported, vetted, and find them a wonderful home."

"Yes, we would like that very much. There's just no way for us to take them with us."

Toni had trusted contacts in Georgia. One of them kindly transported the momma and her blind daughter to Mount Berry Animal Clinic in Rome, Georgia. As Toni raised funds for their care and worked out transportation arrangements to bring them to her home in New Jersey, she made a request of the staff she knew and regarded so highly, "Would it be possible to keep Sugar and

Bella kenneled together? I'm sure it has to be scary and confusing for both of them—especially so for Bella. I think she could really use her mother's comfort."

"We are more than happy to do that."

During their stay, both girls were spayed. They were also treated for hook worms and skin allergies, which were suspected to be ring worm. In addition to the health issues mother and daughter shared, they each had individual concerns.

Sugar had a serious case of heartworm and was carefully treated for it. Fortunately, Bella tested negative for heartworm. However, in addition to being born without eyes, it was discovered that Bella's ear canals were deformed. Even so, she was blessed with hearing.

After receiving much needed veterinary care, the mommy-daughter duo was transported from Georgia to New Jersey where they temporarily settled in the family digs of Toni Diamond. Their new surroundings were different than the backyard that they were so familiar with in Georgia. These two beauties landed at doggy heaven on earth. Not only did they have a lovely and large backyard, but they also had free reign of the house as long as one of their new human friends was home to supervise. They expressed their gratitude for this privilege by having zero accidents inside. Zero!

In addition to plenty of people attention from Toni and her family, Sugar and Bella were also in the company of several other dogs and cats. It was an environment that could—and would—draw out their true personalities and true needs.

Up to this point in her life, Bella had never been alone. Her momma was her comfort and her guide in a world that she could not see. Anytime she was scared or unsure about her surroundings, she did not hesitate to call out with a bark. Her mom came a-runnin' to her side every time.

As the days passed, Bella became more comfortable in her new environment, and more curious. She was, after all, a puppy. Her lack of vision amplified her other senses tenfold. Toni and her family watched in awe over the weeks of her stay as they observed her taking in and memorizing her surroundings as if creating a map in her head.

Discovery is often an adventure of trial and error, and Bella endured her share of mishaps as she put her brave paws forward. She relied on her sense of smell as she came to know her foster family, including all the other animals.

One evening, Bella made her way toward her new friend, Toby, a Yorkshire Terrier, who was cuddling on the couch with Toni's husband. Suddenly, boom! The two bumped heads. Bella was closer to Toby than she thought. Startled by the head butt, Toby barked at Bella as if to say, "Hey! Watch out!" Momma Sugar was up instantly to defend her baby girl.

On another occasion, Bella was gingerly wandering through the house when all of a sudden, crash! She slammed into Toni's cat. Startled out of their wits, the colliding duo sprung into the air with straight, stiff legs and hair standing on ends. When they landed back onto the hardwood floor, both feline and canine scrambled furiously in a panicked effort to dart away from each other. Neither could gain any traction. Bella's sprint to nowhere was followed by a fearful cry. Again, Sugar was there instantly, comforting her daughter with motherly licks.

At first, Sugar was protective of her daughter, but not overly so. She kept a watchful eye from a distance and the moment any person or animal went near Bella, she was on guard. Some made Sugar a little more edgy than others. Mack, Toni's niece's dog was one of them. Mack was actually the most dog-friendly canine in Tony's family, but he weighed a hefty 110 pounds. The big guy was a bit scary for the canine mom who had recently been through so much upheaval with her baby girl.

The longer Sugar and Bella were at Toni's, the more aggressive Sugar became. Mack definitely brought out Sugar's combative side and the two got into a scuffle. Sugar also started a fight with Toni's dog, Buddy. All this aggressive behavior concerned Toni. Clearly, Sugar was stressed. Who could blame her? She had been abandoned by the only family she'd known since she was a puppy herself, and had an unsighted daughter to protect.

Initially, Toni was determined to find a home for this pair together. It seemed natural and logical. She turned to a trainer to help assess the situation. Toni and the trainer separated Sugar from her daughter for a period of time to see what would happen.

After reuniting mom and daughter, the trainer and Toni discussed their observations.

"Toni, Sugar had no aggression issues when she was away from her pup. Her bossy side completely disappeared. I think she puts on a strong front for Bella to protect her baby, but the true Sugar is so sweet! I see how she got her name. She's a Velcro dog. She sticks right by your side. Completely loves human attention and affection."

"You know, it's interesting. Neither of them really missed the other when they were apart, and they were not overjoyed to see each other when they were reunited."

"I recommend that Sugar and Bella part ways. I think it's best for both of them, so they can thrive and live happy lives. They have completely different needs. They are both wonderful dogs, but are in very different stages of their lives."

"Yes, I totally agree. I'm just really surprised by this! I was sure they should be placed in a home together, but they are happier apart."

Bella was just a puppy who wanted to do puppy things: play, chew, discover, learn. Although she had the challenge of no sight, it only took a moment of knowing her to realize that she actually did see the world—just differently than any being with vision. Her big heart oozed love and she was willing to pour it onto every person and animal she encountered.

Sugar, on the other hand, was entering her senior years and wanted to relax. This eight-year-old girl had known only one home her entire life—the backyard of a house. When Toni introduced her to the comforts of the *inside* of a *home* and the warmth of human affection, Sugar was sold. She was completely content being inside and curled up near a gentle, loving person.

Toni changed her plea from one good home for both mom and daughter to two separate homes: one for a senior dog who loved nothing more than human attention and affection; and the other for a blind, but mischievous, pup who would thrive in an active household filled with kids and other dogs. Her pleas and prayers were answered for both girls. Sugar went to Indiana to be an only dog to a wonderful family who showered her with love. Bella found the perfect home with an amazing family in New Hampshire.

When Bella's new family set off to meet Toni half way between New Jersey and New Hampshire to bring Bella to her new home, they were looking forward to a reunion of sorts. Nancy, married with three daughters and four dogs, had adopted from Toni before; a little Schnauzer mix named Mighty. She followed Toni on Facebook and helped her network the dogs that were up for adoption. None of them really spoke to her until she saw a flyer that Toni created about Bella. There was a photo on it of the precious girl cocking her head. Nancy couldn't take her eyes off it. Bella reeled her in. Her visceral presence leaped off the screen and into Nancy's heart.

Nancy texted Bella's photo to her husband while he was away on a business trip, "Ric - I really think she needs our last name. :-)" Nancy knew this girl would fit in perfectly with their family. Since she was home during the day running a very busy household, she was confident she could train Bella. She could take her to classes and work with her at home. Nancy was ready and willing to provide Bella with anything she needed.

Nancy and her three beautiful daughters arrived at the meeting spot in Connecticut to meet and bring their new family member home. There were a lot of smiles and hugs. After getting settled in the car for the trip back, it did not take long for them to realize that Bella was quite vocal and not shy about hiding her feelings. As she sat on the lap of Nancy's oldest daughter, Monika, Bella huffed and puffed most of the way. Her voice was expressive with a mix of excitement for a new adventure and fear of the unknown. Who exactly are these nice people? Where are they taking me?

Her first night in her new home was much the same. Although she went right inside her new crate, she whined and she howled. Monika sighed, "This is going to be a long night!"

The next day, Bella sulked. She went into a corner and wouldn't leave. Bella could no longer rely on the map she created in her head of Toni's home and yard to find her way around. She needed a new map. She also missed Toni. Nancy called her on the phone, "Oh, Toni. We had a rough first night. This morning she found a safe corner and will not leave it. I thought maybe the sound of your voice would make her feel comfortable. Maybe you could even coax her out of the corner?"

Sure enough, the familiar voice motivated Bella. The strategy worked! Nancy made note of key words that Toni used. It occurred to Nancy that Bella responded positively to certain words, while other words invoked no response at all. The young girl had selective hearing.

Over the next few weeks, getting to know Bella was a learning adventure, but it wasn't much different than getting to know any of the other family dogs. They all had unique personalities. Nancy thought Bella would be dependent on her family for everything—from walking on a leash to finding her food and water bowls to finding her bed. It soon became clear that Bella was a bright and mischievous girl whose needs were basic and similar to her canine siblings: food, care, love, and attention.

Bella was a fan of putting her front paws onto the counter and using her nose to snoop for anything interesting. Experimenting with and finding those key words from Toni started coming into play. When Nancy said, "Down!" Bella ignored her and continued counter surfing. When Nancy said, "Off!" Bella responded immediately, and put all four paws on the floor. "Good girl!" Nancy praised her for listening.

The family also learned that all furniture should stay in its place. If anything was moved or added to the mix, Bella didn't hesitate to notify everyone within earshot. Bringing a Christmas tree home threw Bella for a loop. So much so, that the family moved it into a different room—one with a door so Bella wouldn't even know it was there. Certainly it was confusing. Why are you bringing the outdoors inside? It was a question that did not escape Bella.

In short time, Bella created a new map in her head of her new home. With the furniture remaining in place and the Christmas tree strategically relocated, she could find her way around perfectly. She followed walls to guide her and make turns. She zipped up and down the stairs. It was as if she counted. When she reached the bottom, she knew to hook a left. Bella memorized the location of the sliding door and where to scratch to notify her family she wanted to go outside.

Bella also mastered getting up on the kitchen table. Unfortunately, she didn't know how to get down. On Christmas Day, Nancy's middle daughter was sitting at the table, while Bella was on top of it. Nancy asked, "Izzy, do you see what's in front of you?"

"Yes."

"You don't see a problem?"

"Oh, well, yeah, maybe … ."

Mayla giggled. Nancy kissed the top of her youngest daughter's head as she walked toward Izzy to help her help Bella get off of the table.

After getting to know Bella, Nancy's family started suspecting their Border Collie was mixed with a tri-color Basenji. She had the herding talent of the Border Collie down and was great at using her nose to poke all the other dogs and her human siblings. Basenji traits also shined through with her highly mischievous nature accented with a startling, goofy yodel that kept the household entertained.

Soon after Bella's arrival, Nancy enrolled her in basic obedience training. Bella loved going to class. Nancy asked, "Do you want to go to school?" Bella had the same excited reaction every time. She headed to the front door and anxiously awaited the ride to class.

What's training without practice? Nancy called out to the entire canine gang, "Do you want to practice school?" She immediately heard the jingle of five dog tags and the pitter-patter of twenty paws scurrying through the house toward her voice. Bella and the other four dogs all lined up and sat in their spot ready to perform commands: lay down, get up, sit, come, go.

After completing basic obedience, Bella sailed through canine good citizen training. She was not awarded certificates of completion because of her blindness—she earned them fair and square. In fact, Bella aced her canine good citizen test!

All that training never deterred Bella's mischievous charm. Nancy was finding a lot of chewed pencils sprinkled throughout the house. She put on her private investigator hat and caught Bella red-handed opening her daughter's desk drawer, and then sticking her nose inside to steal pencils. It didn't stop there. Bella's strong sense of smell also led to thievery of paper, pens, crayons, and sponges out of the same desk drawer.

Knowing she shouldn't have these things in her mouth, Bella turned her head toward the wall and walked away alongside it in an attempt to conceal the stolen goods from her humans.

She also had a habit of picking up her dog bowl when she was finished eating with a goal to hide it, like a bone. Unfortunately, the bang-bang, bangity-bang of her bowl clanking against the wall as it guided her didn't support a sly getaway.

Despite all the mischief she got into, Bella proved herself to be an excellent, active listener. In addition to Nancy learning and using the key words that Bella already knew, Nancy was able to teach Bella new commands to accommodate her new surroundings. "Watch it!" told Bella to change direction. Hearing, "Up, up, up!" meant to go up the flight of stairs in front of her.

All the commands empowered Bella to enjoy the things she loved with great exuberance. One of those things was the outdoors. Her new home offered her an extremely large yard to explore alongside her canine siblings. Although never outside unsupervised, it warmed Nancy's heart to watch her run free of a leash. Bella was able to exercise her great independence.

When massive snow blanketed New Hampshire during Bella's first winter, Nancy wasn't sure what to expect. In fact, she was a little nervous. Bella took the snow head on—romping through it, eating it. She loved it!

One afternoon, Nancy took Bella out and about. Nancy geared her up with a jacket imprinted with "I'm blind. Please ask to pet." It helped prevent Bella from being startled by people approaching and petting her out of the blue.

The two stopped at their favorite pet store. Soon after they walked through the entrance, an excited voice came over the intercom, "Bella's here!"

Most of the employees knew Bella and loved her. Nancy stopped to say hello.

"Hi, Bella! Hi, Nancy! I have something for you. Well, actually, it's for Bella."

"Oh, my goodness. Thank you!" It was special-made toy: a Kong with cat bells inside so Bella could find it.

As Nancy showed Bella her new toy, a gentleman approached, "She's really blind?"

"Yes, she is. Actually, she doesn't have any eyes."

He reacted with great intrigue and awe, "Whoa! Can I look?"

Nancy encouraged him, "Yes, go ahead. The sockets are there, she has eyelashes and full drainage, but she does not have eyeballs. She was born that way. We had her lids sewn shut, and give her eyes a lot of love. We clean them and kiss them."

"That's amazing. What an amazing dog!"

Smiling proudly, Nancy agreed, "She really is remarkable. The nice thing about being a handicapped dog—and I really don't like the word handicapped—is that nobody can tell them what ability they are missing. In the world we live in, a blind person is constantly being reminded of what he or she is missing. Bella has no clue what she's missing. She thinks everybody walks into walls."

"You make a really good point," The gentleman smiled, let Bella smell his hand, and gave her some kind pets and rubs.

The pet store worker who gifted Bella chimed in, "I fell in love with Bella the instant I met her. She has an effervescent personality. It's hard to explain, but she really draws people in."

The gentleman smiled brightly. "She certainly does!" He then became contemplative and looked to Nancy as he continued soothing Bella with kind pets, "I bet a lot of people would not even consider adopting a blind dog."

"Sadly, you're right. They see them as lacking sight. The truth is, Bella may have been born without eyes, but the world she sees has no limits. Dogs like Bella who are supposedly lacking in something, whether it be vision, hearing, a leg, or something else, have a lot to teach us. And, boy, has she taught my family some great lessons."

"What do you think is the greatest lesson you've learned from her?" He was intrigued.

"She's taught my family that life is limitless. Just like so many other families, we have challenges with school, work, health. Bella demonstrates day in and day out that these challenges need to be faced and tackled head on."

"Completely inspiring!" The gentleman couldn't get enough of Bella.

"If she could talk, I know exactly what'd she'd say."

"What's that?" The store worker asked.

"She would tell us all that every animal deserves a chance. Every animal has something to offer our hearts and our minds. Every animal is capable of teaching, amazing, and inspiring us. Every single one."

"What a pleasure to meet such an inspiration as you, Miss Bella," The gentleman gave Bella one last scratch behind her ears and went on his way.

When Nancy returned home, she told her husband all about the heartwarming trip she and Bella had the pet store.

"Bella is an unexpected gift, Nancy. No doubt about it," Ric gave Bella some loving pets.

"She has a certain innocence and bliss about her. It comes from not knowing what she's missing. It's different than naivety because Bella is wise. Very wise. She has seen darkness, but she has also seen light. She enlightens others with her limitless imagination."

"She's masterful," Ric smiled admirably at Bella, and then at his wife.

Nancy laughed and nodded in fast agreement, "This is the world, and she owns it!"

16

VOLUNTEERING FOR AN ANIMAL SHELTER OR RESCUE IS PAWSIBLE

Chance morphed from a clumsy, silly juvenile into a confident, adult leader after Filbert passed away. Initially, our loss put this sensitive boy into a deep depression. He was uncharacteristically serene and sad. His wide, happy grin vanished. After two weeks of grieving, I awoke to a changed dog. He suddenly let it go. Permanently. His wide, happy grin returned, and his bond with Parker solidified. In fact, they became a truly bonded pair. Anywhere Chance went, Parker was sure to follow.

Parker idolized Chance. It's like nothing I have ever witnessed. Parker was obsessed. He was Chance's personal groomer, constantly licking his ears. Chance took great pride in his new role as alpha dog. No longer a student, he was now the teacher.

Along with his wide, happy grin, Chance's high energy returned. Playful as ever, Chance loved to challenge Parker in tug of war. Throwing a Frisbee turned into games of keep-away from Parker. Although Parker couldn't quite grasp catching the flying toy, he was quick in his attempts to steal it.

Parker was a thief. He especially loved to steal balls. He had a knack for finding them at the park or on walks and proudly carried them in his mouth all the way home. When he came in possession of baseballs, he incessantly chewed and gnawed on them until they were completely defaced. Any curiosity I ever had about the innards of a baseball were satisfied by Parker.

My Corgi-mix was good and quick at fetching balls. It was a great way to expend his high energy level, which rivaled Chance's. Catching a fly ball? Well, that was another story. It took him two years to realize he was a dog, not a human, and was never going to be able to catch a pop fly with his two front paws.

Parker joined Chance and I on our short-distance runs. His low-rider Corgi legs maxed out at two miles.

The three of us moved to Playa del Rey. We lived exactly one mile from the beach. It wasn't hard for these two to fall in love with the sound of waves and the fresh ocean breeze. Getting in the water? No, thank you, Mom. A nice walk along the sand? Yes, please!

Along with the move, I had an unrelenting desire to do something significant with my life to make a difference in the world. Lost and homeless dogs were barking my name.

In January 2013, my friend, Brooke, introduced me to her friend, Sarah, who introduced me to Jennifer. Jennifer was the volunteer coordinator for Project Picture for Lu Parker Project, a non-profit organization dedicated to improving the lives of homeless animals and at-risk youth through education, the arts, and community projects.

The goal of Project Picture was to take and share beautiful photographs of adoptable animals at high-risk of being euthanized due to overcrowding at South Los Angeles Animal Shelter. A great photo can make all the difference in getting dogs, as well as other shelter animals, adopted.

Volunteers met every few weeks at the shelter. All of us were true animal lovers with an unyeilding desire to find these wonderful animals forever homes.

Some of the volunteers were extremely talented photographers. Others of us handled the dogs. We pulled them from the kennels and walked them to the play yard to release some energy and give them lots of love, attention, and affection.

As dog handlers, we did our best to bring out their true personalities for the photographers to capture. Rather than taking quick snapshots of sad, scared dogs behind bars, the photographers took stunning photographs of the dogs, as well as cats, bunnies, and even turtles available for adoption.

After spending part of the day with the animals, we would network them by sharing their gorgeous pictures on social media and email. It worked! People were drawn to the colorful images of happy dogs showing off their personalities. The photographs inspired and increased adoptions at South Los Angeles Animal Shelter.

The shelter offered training classes to those volunteers who wanted to handle the dogs. I will never forget the first dog I pulled from her kennel on my own and walked to the play yard to be photographed.

Dolly was a stunning Rottweiler mix. She was only five years old and on the small side for a Rottie. For two months she had been overlooked at the shelter, perhaps because she was quiet, black, and had a tendency to hang in the back of her kennel. As a result, she was at the top of the list to be euthanized.

When I stepped up to her kennel and spoke to her, she kindly responded. Her head tilted with listening ears. Her eyes were wanting and gentle. She spoke volumes without making a peep.

The shelter worker unlocked the kennel for me. I put the leash around Dolly and we walked side by side to the back play yard. The path we took was lined on both sides with full kennels of barking, howling, and whining dogs. Dolly took it all in stride. She walked with quiet confidence. She didn't flinch or utter a single bark. She was lovely. Along our 200 yard stroll, I fell in love with her.

Marissa, photographer extraordinaire of De La Doggies photography and dog walking services, captured Dolly's beauty perfectly. I shared her photograph on social media and networked her like crazy. The thought of this amazing animal being killed had me on edge. I couldn't sleep. I was obsessed with finding a rescue to pull her out of the shelter, or better yet, someone to adopt her. I solicited help on Facebook:

Rescue? Adopt? Foster? If anyone can step up to save this girl's life … she is simply wonderful. Dolly has a calm, peaceful disposition. Just being in her presence soothes the soul. I met her yesterday at South Los Angeles Animal Shelter, CA. For two months, she has been overlooked. If you cannot adopt, please foster or rescue. Please share Dolly. Thank you.

My request and prayers were answered. An amazing woman named Melody stepped up to foster. She was a Los Angeles Animal Services (LAAS) foster with two dogs and a cat of her own. She typically fostered kittens, but was moved by my pleas to help Dolly.

Filled with hope and excitement, I felt compelled to go to South LA shelter to see Dolly and tell her the big news in person. We scored some one-on-one time together in the play yard, and I told her, "Guess what, Dolly? You are getting out of here tomorrow! A wonderful woman is going to pick you up and take good care of you for a little while. We are going to find you a forever home. I promise. I know the perfect family is just waiting for you." She smiled and wagged her long tail. I am certain she understood my every word.

As a LAAS foster, Melody was able to pull Dolly from South LA shelter the next morning. She took a snapshot of a bright-eyed, smiling Dolly on her freedom ride, and sent it to me. What a thrill!

First stop for Dolly was the groomer. Second stop was an adoption event where everyone who met her adored her. She proved herself to be great with kids, as well as other dogs.

When I got to work on Monday, I shared Dolly's story with my co-workers. One of them expressed great interest in meeting and possibly adopting her, so I reached out to Melody.

After only a few days in foster care, Melody introduced Dolly to my co-worker and her boyfriend. They decided to keep her for the weekend for a trial run. Near the end of the weekend, my co-worker shared some photographs of a happy Dolly with Melody and I through email. Melody sent a reply:

"Those are AMAZING!! I'm never getting her back, am I?!!"

She didn't.

My co-worker and her boyfriend fell in love with Dolly and renamed her Posey. After spending sixty days and sixty nights behind bars on a cement floor, this beautiful Rottweiler mix barely escaped death. In that escape, she found the perfect forever home, just as I promised.

Melody wrote me an update shortly after the adoption was final:

"I can't tell you how happy Dolly looked outside her new home in her great new neighborhood. She is going to have such a great, adventurous life. She has done more in the past two weeks than her entire life, I'm sure! From daycare to grooming to car rides to movie sets to The Grove to a road trip this weekend up north [to San Francisco]. Wow! What a beautiful soul Dolly is. I'm so glad I got to be a small part of her life. She really touched me. So, thank you for what you do. Posting her and pleading for her got me to notice her. For whatever reason, I knew I had to help her. I just didn't think it [finding her a forever home] would be so fast!"

My heart was full.

When I started volunteering, the most common question family and friends asked was, "How can you handle being in the shelter with all those sad dogs barking? I couldn't do it. How do you do it?"

My answer is always the same, "It's not about me. It's about them."

In helping homeless, as well as lost dogs, I found my calling. There is a quote I have come to love as I've devoted more of my time to helping animals:

"Saving the life of one animal may not change the world, but the world will surely change for that one animal."

—Karen Davison, Author, *A Dog's Guide to Humans*

CATS HAVE PAWS, TOO

17

SURVIVING AGAINST THE ODDS IS PAWSIBLE

Robyn lived in a high rise apartment in Edgewater, New Jersey. It is a picturesque community that sits along the Hudson River with views of New York City. Every day, she went for a walk around her neighborhood and made a point to bring cat food with her. She had a soft spot for feral cats and often crossed paths with one or two along her route.

One day, she came across a six month old feral kitten. He was living behind a dumpster in the parking lot of Robyn's building. She fed the kitten, who took a quick liking to her gentle kindness. Over the next couple of weeks, the two developed a routine. Every afternoon, Robyn whistled for him. The kitten came out of hiding to greet her and get nourishment.

The neighborhood children caught on to Robyn's routine with the kitten quickly. It was nearing Christmastime. Bundled in parkas, mittens, and scarves, they gathered around and watched adoringly as the little one ate the food Robyn fed him.

"Miss Robyn? Does the kitten have a name?" One of the young girls was curious.

"No, not yet. Would you like to give him a name?"

"Yes, he's so cute! He needs a name."

One of the boys nodded firmly in agreement. Robyn laughed and smiled at the boy.

"That's a great idea!" She cheered. "Can any of you think of one?"

"How about Rudolph? Like Rudolph the Red-Nosed Reindeer?" Another girl excitedly suggested.

"Yeah! Yeah!" The kids exclaimed in unison.

"That's perfect," Robyn agreed.

Days later, Robyn didn't see her new friend. She hoped he was fine. Two, three, and four days passed with still no sign of him. Concern simmered within her. When a week went by without so much as a glimpse of the little Rudolph, Robyn's heart overflowed with worry. Why wasn't he coming out? Where was he?

Late one night, she couldn't keep her mind off him. She threw a coat on over her pajamas and went outside to look for him. She frantically searched everywhere. Suddenly, she stopped in her tracks and listened. What was that sound? Straining her ears she heard a small animal cry. It was coming from the direction of her car, which happened to be parked near the dumpster he often hid behind. She bustled over, and then crouched down to look underneath her vehicle. There he was! Of all the cars parked in the lot, Rudolph picked hers for shelter.

The little guy didn't look well. His body was limp and his tongue was hanging out. "Hi, Rudolph. Hello. Come here, little one. Please come out, Rudy." She tried to encourage her weak friend to move toward her. He didn't budge.

Robyn needed a new tactic. Determined, she rose to her feet and looked around. She spotted a long stick. Perfect! Getting back down on her hands and knees as she arrived back at her vehicle, she spoke calmly and sweetly to Rudy. She ever-so-gently used the stick to nudge him toward her. With much patience and persistence, Rudy finally started to inch toward Robyn.

When he was close enough, she carefully reached in to pick him up. "Easy, boy." He trusted her to pick him up, and she trusted him to not bite her. With Rudy safely in her arms, she got into her car and took him to an all-night animal hospital. The closest one she could find was 40 minutes away.

Robyn sat nervously in the exam room while the veterinarian checked over the fading kitten. "He is very sick. Who's cat is this?"

With tears welling in her eyes, "He's an outdoor cat. He lives near my apartment. I feed him every day."

"Since he is so ill, I am recommending that we put him down. Between tests to determine what is causing this and bringing him back to health, it is going to be quite expensive."

"I will pay the bills. Please. Please try to save him."

Hesitant, the doctor nodded, "Okay. We will do our best. But, please know that if he happens to bite any of the techs, he will have to be put down. He could have rabies."

Nodding her head, she looked at the ailing kitten with tears, and then up at the vet, "I understand."

Rudy stayed at the veterinary hospital for about two and a half weeks. The bills shot up quickly and reached over $1,500. When she called for an update, the vet continued to advise her to put him down.

"Ma'am, he's not eating, and I still have not been able to determine the root cause of his illness. His blood tests continue to come back abnormal. I suspect he may have eaten poison, but I cannot be sure."

Through a flood of tears, she begged him, "No. No! Please don't give up on him. I'm not giving up on him!" She hung up the phone, grabbed her car keys, and drove to him.

When she arrived, one of the staff brought Robyn to Rudy. She gently stroked him and cheered him on, "Come on, Rudy! Come on. You can pull through this. I know it. I believe in you." He cocked his head and looked at her as if to say, "Please take me home."

At that moment, Robyn knew what she had to do.

"I'm going to take him home now."

"I would highly advise against that. You have other animals, right?"

"Yes, I have a couple of cats."

"Like I said before, I don't know what's causing this. It might be poisoning, but he could also have a virus. He could infect your other animals."

Robyn looked at Rudy. She studied him with thoughtful eyes for a moment, and then looked up at the vet with calm and confidence, "I think he's going to be okay. I'm going to take very good care of him, and I believe he will pull through this."

Robyn and Rudy headed home. She carried him straight into the bathroom where she kept him comfortably quarantined and away from her other animals just in case he was infectious. She diligently tended to Rudy's care, and gave him lots of love and attention. Two weeks later, Rudy was a happy, healthy house cat.

Rudy is now 22 years old and still living in that high rise with Robyn. He survived against all odds. The vet gave up on him, but Robyn never did.

Along with Rudy, Robyn has three other cats, Sesame, Shilo and Mackensie, as well as a Shih Tzu dog, Sophie. Robyn continues to be a savior to the feral cats in her neighborhood. Many have been trapped, neutered, and released. There is one feral cat in particular that is special. When she takes Sophie for walks, she blows a whistle and out comes Mackensie's momma, who happily follows her around the neighborhood as she walks her dog.

18-1

SUPPORTING CAT RESCUES IS PAWSIBLE

Deb, a Jersey girl working in Los Angeles as a TV producer, grew up around all sorts of animals and loved each and every one. As a young professional, she finally reached a place in her life where she could give a pet the wonderful life any animal deserves. Her only obstacle was her roommate, who was a professional soprano singer. She brought the topic up again. "Hey, roomie. Have you given any more thought to having a cat around? I'd really love to adopt one!"

"I'm cool with it, Deb. As long as it's declawed."

After doing some research, Deb found a cat named Gigi. Much to her great disappointment, her application was not approved. For whatever reason, the rescue didn't feel they were a perfect match. Deb didn't let this dissuade her. Searching for a pet is often like dating. It's best to be patient. The right one will come along. Sure enough, a week later she came across a cat who was available for adoption from a rescue in San Francisco.

Very excited, she told her roommate, "I found the perfect cat! You're not going to believe this story. He's a Persian that was left at the vet over a $300 vet bill. His owner just abandoned him there. Do you believe that? The rescue is arranging transport to LA for me. They actually just called and are probably getting in the car right this moment. I cannot wait!"

"Deb, sorry, but I changed my mind. I just don't want a cat here. I cannot risk my voice. I've lived with cats before, and my range goes down an octave. I guess because of my allergies."

Deb's eyes welled up with tears, "He is in a crate on his way down here now. Why didn't you tell me sooner?"

She pulled herself together, and then called the woman fostering him with the news.

"I am so sorry to tell you this, Darlene, but my roommate changed her mind. She won't let me get a cat. I'm moving out, but it will take a bit of time. So, if you find another home for Shanti, please … just … go ahead and make sure he gets a wonderful home."

"Deb, you are the perfect person to care for Shanti. I will continue fostering him. Go ahead and get moved. When you're settled, we'll make arrangements to get him to you."

"Really?"

"Yes, really! We've had him this long, what's another few weeks?"

"Oh, thank you so much, Darlene!"

A month later, Deb happily moved out of the apartment she shared and moved into one of her own so she could adopt Shanti. She drove two hours north to pick up Shanti in Bakersfield, California. As soon as she laid eyes on him she squealed with excitement, "That's my cat!" It was love at first sight.

"A new home deserves a new name. You need a good Italian name." With part Italian ancestry, Deb was also obsessed with a show that was popular at the time, *Growing Up Gotti*. "Hmmm. Gotti. Gotti! What do you think, beautiful boy?"

Gotti

Deb and Gotti settled into a new routine together nicely. Unfortunately, Deb started working a lot of hours and noticed that Gotti was pretty lonely. He was only about four or five years old, but always seemed to be getting sick. As fate would have it, Deb got a phone call from Darlene.

"Deb, lots has happened since we last spoke. I moved to Reno and started my own rescue! We have some Himalayans, and one of them is pregnant. I thought of you right away and was wondering if you would like to adopt one of the kittens?"

"That's so crazy. I was just thinking about getting a companion for Gotti. He's so lonely. Are they seal point Himalayans?"

"Yes, they are."

"Great, I want one!"

There were three females in the litter. Deb adopted one, while a woman named Holly adopted the other two. Darlene's rescue, Divine Felines Purebred Rescue (DFPR), cared for the litter of three for six months, and then planned to have them transported to their new homes. While Deb and Holly waited for their babies to grow healthy and big enough to travel, Darlene sent photos of the growing kitties. They all became an extended family.

The day finally arrived. "Gotti, Gotti! Come here, boy. I've got a surprise for you! Meet your sister, Gucci." A light of excitement sparked Gotti's gorgeous green eyes and he happily welcomed Gucci into the family.

Gucci

Gucci wasn't as receptive to Gotti's affections. In fact, she wanted nothing to do with him—or, so she pretended. One day, not long after her arrival, Gucci started following Gotti around the apartment. Feeling as if he was being watched as he strolled, Gotti repeatedly stopped and turned to look behind him. Each time he did, Gucci stopped in her tracks and pretentiously looked away. Deb smiled and laughed, "I saw that!" At that moment, the fuzzy felines became best friends.

18-2

BECOMING A CERTIFIED THERAPY DOG IS PAWSIBLE

With Gotti and Gucci so bonded, Deb started feeling ignored and lonely. She decided to expand her family and get a dog. When she was a child, her aunt and uncle had a Cocker Spaniel named Beau. Deb loved that dog. As an adult, she often volunteered at Camp Cocker Rescue and the Carson Animal Shelter in southern Los Angeles County. Every time she volunteered, she checked the computer system for Cocker Spaniels that were up for adoption at area shelters.

On one of her searches, she came across a photo of an adorable Cocker Spaniel at the Castaic Animal Shelter in northern Los Angeles County. A few days later she checked the system again. When he wasn't listed anymore, she thought, "Good! He found a home."

Two weeks later, Deb did her usual Cocker Spaniel search. "I can't believe it."

"What's up?" One of the shelter employees was standing nearby.

"This super adorable Cocker Spaniel I found listed two weeks ago is back at Castaic shelter. I'm going to call."

With quick fingers, Deb dialed, thinking this might be a sign. "Hi! I'm a volunteer at the Carson shelter. I was looking in the system and there's a Cocker Spaniel that looks like he was adopted a couple weeks ago, but is now back at your shelter. What can you tell me about him?" She gave the woman on the other end of the phone the cutie's ID number.

"The notes here say he was returned because he wanted too much human attention."

"Hmmm. Well, cockers need their people. They're people dogs! I guess it wasn't a good match. I totally want him, but, I can't get up there until Saturday. It's an hour-and-a-half drive for me. If someone else wants him before I can get up there, that's great. If not, I will be there Saturday. I promise!" She made sure to leave her name and number, especially because Castaic is a high kill shelter.

A couple days later, the woman at the Castaic shelter pegged Deb as soon as she came in. "Let's go get Copper so you can meet."

"Yes, let's. Hey, do you know his story? I know he was returned, but how did he end up here the first time?"

"He's a foreclosure dog. The original owners couldn't afford him anymore. Since this is his second time back, you are his last chance. No one else has expressed interest."

Deb looked at Copper. "You are adorable! But, you're a little chunky. It's okay. I have to lose ten pounds. You have to lose ten pounds. We'll do it together!" As the new pair exited the shelter, Deb watched Copper waddle and smiled with satisfaction. She just saved a life.

Copper

On Copper's first few nights in his new home, Deb stayed with him to make sure he felt safe and comfortable. On his fourth night, she went out for a few hours to have dinner with friends. Shortly after she got home, there was a knock on her door. It was a neighbor.

"Hi, there. What's up?"

"Hey, Deb. Your dog was howling nonstop while you were gone."

"Oh no! Are you serious?"

"Yeah. It was pretty bad. We were really worried 'cuz we thought something was wrong. I mean, we thought he might be hurt or even dying because he just wouldn't stop. We tried breaking in to calm him down, but your place is tight."

"Oh, my gosh. I'm so sorry! Thank you so much for trying to help him." Deb pressed her hands against her cheeks as she turned to look at Copper with a worried brow. He gazed up at her with drooping, apologetic eyes.

Kneeling down to comfort him with soothing chin rubs and light, long back caresses, she asked, "Oh, Copper buddy, what's wrong? You don't like being alone, do you? We'll fix this. Don't you worry."

Knowing his separation anxiety issues were severe, Deb immediately called upon a trainer with great hope of easing Copper's anxious ways. With training in progress, Deb was still leery about leaving Copper alone. One afternoon, Deb had her next door neighbor watch him while she went out on a work errand.

"Please, please don't leave him alone. Not even for a second."

"No worries, Deb. I'll watch him like a hawk!"

After hanging with Copper for a while, Deb's neighbor went downstairs to her apartment to quickly grab some food. She figured Copper had been great so far, he would be okay for a minute alone. Getting side tracked, the neighbor stepped outside—right below Deb's second story window—to chat with some friends.

Scratching and banging noises caught the attention of one of the friends. He looked up and pointed, "Oh. My. Gosh."

"OH, NO! COPPER!" Deb's neighbor couldn't believe her eyes. Copper had nudged a barely cracked open window fully open with his nose, and was now standing on a weak flower ledge. Before she could even think to run upstairs, he catapulted himself from the second story in a desperate need to escape solitude and fly to the presence of people.

Landing in the grass on his bottom, which still had almost twenty pounds of extra cushion, Copper appeared to everyone to be okay. Deb's roommate ran up the street to get a friend who was a doctor to check him more closely. When it was determined that Copper was miraculously fine, they gave Deb a call.

"He's totally fine, Deb. Really! I'm so sorry this happened, but he really is okay. Just a little bruise on his butt."

Deb took Copper to her local veterinary office to be checked and cleared of any injuries. She explained to her veterinarian, "Copper has major separation anxiety and, obviously, he is a bit overweight. I think his original owners didn't leave him alone very often. Every time they did, they fed him. Every time he made noise, they fed him. Basically, he was getting positive reinforcement to bark, howl, and eat too much!"

Despite Copper's separation anxiety, Deb knew she had a wonderful dog on her hands. While continuing behavior training to resolve the anxiety issue, Deb decided to have him tested for the Canine Good Citizen award. "Let's go see just how awesome you are, Copper!"

At the testing facility she chatted with the couple in line in front of her, who had had their dog for years. They were up next, and Deb cheered them on, "Good luck!"

Their dog failed the test miserably. "Oh, boy. Let's shake these nerves, Copper." She took a deep breath and they hit the testing floor.

The group running the testing for the Canine Good Citizen award was Love On 4 Paws. The trainer that tested Copper was impressed, "Congratulations! Copper passed with flying colors. Great job, Copper!"

"Oh, my gosh! On his first run, too. He is amazing! I adopted him just a couple weeks ago."

"Wow! Really? He is definitely amazing! I wonder if you would be interested in testing him for volunteering at the hospital—doing bed visits with the patients? I think he would be fantastic."

Beaming with pride, Deb didn't need to think long about it, "I think that would be so cool. What do we need to do?"

"I will get you a list of things therapy dogs are tested on. You can practice with him and when you think he's ready, just go have him tested. I think he'll do great!"

She was right. Copper became a therapy dog. He and Deb started volunteering at local hospitals two or three times a month.

"Guess where we're going today, Copper?" Copper slipped into his little Therapy Dog vest and off they went to do bed visits at the hospital.

"Hi, there!" Deb greeted a young girl. "This is Copper. He wanted to come in and visit with you for a little while. Would that be okay?"

The child's pale face beamed with excitement as she nodded.

"My name is Deb. What's yours?" She asked as she placed a cotton sheet for Copper on the child's bed.

"Emmy." The young girl could hardly contain herself as Deb lifted Copper to sit next to his new friend on her hospital bed. "Hi, Copper." She reached out to pet him and he nuzzled right into her hand, clearly in heaven receiving love and pets. Emmy giggled and barely noticed the nurse come into her room. *(NOTE: "Emmy" is a fictitious name used for confidentiality.)*

Copper continued to cuddle and happily accept his new pal's touches.

As the nurse prepared a shot, she smiled at the scene, "Hi Emmy. Who are your friends?"

"This is Deb and Copper." Her grin was wide. "Isn't he so cute?" She petted him dotingly, while Copper remained calm with a wagging tail.

"Adorable! Such a sweet dog and nice new friend. I'm going to give you a little shot in the arm, but you just keep playing with Copper and you won't even notice."

"Okay," Emmy tensed, but continued holding onto Copper—holding him and looking into his eyes for comfort. Deb looked on proudly.

"All done! You did great, Emmy!"

"Good job!" Deb chimed in. "I have something for you for being such a brave girl."

"Really? What is it?"

Deb pulled out what looked like baseball cards, and then handed one to Emmy.

"Cool! Copper, this card has your picture on it. You must be famous!" Emmy held the card up to Copper's face and moved it from side to side.

Deb laughed, "He will always be with you. There are some fun facts about him written on the back, too."

Emmy kissed Copper's card, and then looked at Copper and hugged him, "I love you!"

18-3

TRAP, NEUTER, RELEASE IS PAWSIBLE

In June 2012, a co-worker knocked on Deb's office door. "Hey, Deb! You up for a little break? You being the cat expert you are, we could really use your help."

"This sounds interesting. What's going on?"

"There are a bunch of cats on the 'Let's Make a Deal' set. Well, cats and kittens. They are wreaking havoc. Super cute, but they're taking potty breaks on set. And, who knew such small creatures could be so noisy? Lots of meowing going on! It's really disrupting taping."

"Oh, boy. Yeah, show me the way."

Arriving on set, Deb and her co-worker started counting cats.

"Looks like there's about four or five?"

"Five, I think. There's a mom and dad, plus a few kittens. The mom is nearly as tiny as her kitties." The co-worker waved Deb over to show her a hole in the wall. They both crouched down and Deb peered through it. The hole led straight out to the parking lot.

"I'm so worried they'll get hit by a car. We should trap them. I'll get permission from the studios, and then give Nora from Kitty Bungalow a call. They do TNR."

"What's that?"

"Trap, neuter, release."

Deb made sure to be present when Kitty Bungalow arrived with traps. She didn't want any of the cats ending up at a shelter. Feral kittens would never stand a chance of getting out. Most cats have low chances of making it out of a shelter alive as it is.

When the Kitty Bungalow team arrived, Deb approached one of the gentlemen, "I would love to foster these kittens and find them homes. Would that be possible?"

"They'll need to be tamed."

"I can do that."

"They're all yours."

By the next day all of the eight-week-old kittens were caught, along with mom and dad. The family was taken to Kitty Bungalow to get spayed and neutered. Set workers sealed up the hole on stage that led outside.

Later that day, the loud speaker came on. "Deb to Stage 1. Deb to Stage 1."

Uh-oh, Deb thought. Stage 1 was not her stage. Something was wrong.

When Deb arrived to Stage 1, she heard a shrill cry. Deb looked around trying to figure out where the noise was coming from. She heard the distressing sound again, and ran frantically toward the repaired wall. "Oh, my gosh! Is there a kitten trapped in there?"

A set worker unrepaired his repair work to get the kitten out. When the wall opened up, the clever one managed to bamboozle everyone, again. She cunningly snuck by and was back on the loose. The chase was on!

Grown men were running madly from one set to another chasing a fuzzy two pound kitten. "She's on Set 2. No, wait! She's off toward Set 4. Now, she's by Set 6! We're running! We're gonna get her!" They even got nets out, but this little smarty was no butterfly. She was a weaving bullet! No one could catch her. They gave up for the day.

Deb worked late that night and spotted the little one by her car. Thinking and moving quickly in an effort to finally outsmart the clever kitty, Deb grabbed one of the traps provided by Kitty Bungalow, moved it near her car and put some food in it. Although she didn't catch her on the spot, she left work that night with a good feeling. Sure enough, she was in the trap the next morning. Deb named her Nala.

After being spayed and neutered, Deb released mom and dad back out into the world. The two were extremely feral and taming them wasn't going to happen. The four kittens were another story. One of Deb's neighbors had a spare room. The two of them teamed up with their mutual friend, Julie, to tame all four kittens. The three women worked with them every day by holding and playing with them, and introducing them to other people. It was hard, but they were all dedicated to the task.

As soon as she thought the kittens were ready, Deb contacted Cats At The Studios rescue group. They agreed to let them participate in their weekly adoption event in Woodland Hills to help the kittens find forever homes. The cuties were all quickly adopted. A few weeks later, Deb got a call from the rescue. The woman who adopted Nala was at her wits end. She couldn't take anymore of Nala's bad behavior. She was pooping and peeing everywhere. Deb called the woman directly.

"I can't afford this. She ruined three beds and comforters."

"I'm so sorry to hear that," Deb was sympathetic.

"Also, I think she is half blind. She is constantly bumping into things."

"Really?" Deb was stunned. This was the same cat that outsmarted all those grown men chasing her. "Have you taken her to the vet?"

"No."

Deb sensed there was no way to make it work for them. "I'll take her."

Deb with her crew: Gotti, Nala, Gucci and Copper (left to right)

Unsure about what she was stepping into, Deb brought her home. "Do you remember this place, Nala?" She knew exactly where she was! She stepped into the kitchen and then darted to the bathroom where Deb had kept her most of the time during her taming period. Gucci was quite happy to see her cuddle buddy and greeted her with a long moving nuzzle. Gotti, ruler of the household, looked on with indifference. Copper was thrilled to have so many friends in the same room.

"So what's going on with you, Nala?" Deb pressed her forehead against Nala's and then sat back. Her eyes were extremely dilated. After giving her a couple of days to readjust, Deb chatted with a friend, "She doesn't cause any problems at my place. She's happy and content. I think she was really freaked out at that lady's house. Her acting out was her way of communicating that she didn't want to be there. It wasn't the right home for her."

After fostering Nala for several months, the ever-so-sweet and affectionate girl found her forever home right down the street. She was also reunited with one of her brothers. Deb's neighbor, who adopted Nala's brother earlier that year, decided to adopt Nala, too.

18-4

HONORING A FURRY FRIEND IS PAWSIBLE

A couple of months after Nala was adopted, Deb became alarmed when Gotti started losing weight. He had a history of hypertension and heart problems, but those were under control. She kept a close eye on him. After an exam, the vet gave Deb his diagnosis, "I'm so sorry to tell you that Gotti is anemic and in the beginning stages of renal failure."

Deb's heart sank. She tried to keep his weight up, but with each visit to the vet he weighed less and less. He got down to four pounds. On September 15, 2013, Gotti passed away.

The world crashed for Deb that day. She couldn't sleep. She couldn't eat. She didn't feel human. Not typically a cuddler, Copper kissed and cozied with Deb to ease her heavy pain. He offered Gucci his affections, too. Gotti's passing was a great loss for Gucci. She missed him deeply. As time went by, the pain lessoned and she started enjoying getting all of Deb's kitty attentions.

Even with an aching heart, Deb continued to foster cats and kittens. As of this writing, she was caring for four 9-week-old kittens and thinking about taking in another one. Her philosophy is simple, "There are always kittens and I have an extra room, so why not foster?"

TRIBUTES TO GOTTI

To my Gott Gott-

I miss you more than words could ever express. It's like a part of me is missing and it's hard to face the fact that it's never coming back. I know I rescued you 8 years ago, but in reality, you really rescued me.

Gotti

I knew you were my kitty the second I saw your picture on Pet Finder- the one where your tongue was sticking out and you had an under-bite that made you look gangster- thus, how you got your name Gotti. When I picked you up and saw you for the first time, I melted. I knew that instant that I was your human.

We've had so much fun together over the last 8 years, haven't we? From TV talk show office visits, where you peed on a certain staff member's chair to neighborhood parties that I brought you to so everybody could pet you to our plane and train rides to visit family and friends in Vegas, NYC, New Jersey, Philly and Chicago. You were one well-traveled kitty, and I'm glad I got to experience it all with you.

We also had some really funny times together. Remember when Gucci was a kitten and came home for the first time? You loved her instantly, but she tried to play off like she hated you—until I caught her secretly following you around the apartment. Remember the time that you were groomed and she hissed at you for two weeks straight because you smelled so different? Remember the time at Aunt Rhonda's when you were sitting on her white furry rug and we thought we had lost you because you blended right in? How about doing the "I'm a cat, I'm a cat, I'm a kitty cat" dance? Or, all of the many TV auditions and TV sets I dragged you to? Is it sad that my cat has a better demo reel than me?

You were my judge on whether or not a guy was good enough to date. If you approached them and they lit up and tried to pet you, they were in. If they ignored you, they were instantly out. By the way, I really should have listened to you when you peed all over a certain boyfriend's clothes—several times. Sorry about that. I figured it out eventually!

I will never forget your silent meow, or the smile you put on my face every time I walked through the door. My favorite moment of the day would be in the morning when I would wake up to 3 sleeping animals and say "Ok, everybody up!" and see you and two other adoring faces looking at me, so excited to start their day. I also loved when I would work on my laptop and you would lay on my back to try to help.

You were just such a cool and gentle cat. You welcomed every foster kitten I brought in the house with open arms, and there were A LOT! You ruled my apartment without ever being mean. Gucci and Copper just automatically knew who was boss. SO very Garfield and Odie!

Gucci misses you too. She was your little sister, your partner in crime and you always took such good care of her. Don't worry she is trying her hardest to make me smile like you told her to do once you were gone, and she is doing a very good job.

I miss you, Gott, and hope you are feeling better in kitty heaven. I will never have another cat—or friend—quite like you. I'm so blessed you found me and I was able to share eight amazing years with you. It wasn't enough, but 100 years wouldn't have been enough either.

Forever in Our Hearts, Gotti

Love,

Mom Deb

* * *

No matter how sick or frail he got, he never failed to follow me around, hoping I'd stop a moment to play with him. He always remained a kitten at heart.

-Mike Snyder

I remember when Gotti came to visit me in my tiny apartment in NYC. I was not a cat person, but during that short visit, I fell in love. He was so soft and fluffy, quiet and disarming. He was able to bring life to my place, so much so I felt his absence deeply after he left. I will always remember Gotti because he is the cat who turned me into a cat lover.

-Stacie L. Nice

I remember the time Gotti and Gucci stole my car rental keys. They were playing with them & they lost them. I had to have the rental company come out and bring me another set of keys before my car got towed . Lol !!!!

Drue said she wanted to marry Gotti when she first met him because she loved him so much :) We tried to pack him in our suitcase at 4am before our flight back to New Jersey, but Deb woke up and said we couldn't steal him. Rest in Peace Gotti. You were very loved.

-Dawn and Drue Fitzgerald

* * *

The 1st time I met Gotti was during a Christmas visit. I'm allergic to cats, so Deb said "Don't pet him!" and left the room. Gotti immediately jumped on my lap and I couldn't help but pet such a sweetheart. Unfortunately, my eyes swelled up and I couldn't see for the rest of the day, but petting such a love bug was worth it.

Love and miss you Gotti!

Michelle Leavenworth

When Deb rescued Gotti we were working together at a popular TV talk show. She would bring him to work every day in a pink sequined bag and he wasn't just her cat—he was an extension of her. I was never really a cat person, but how can you not love a cat with such a cute face!

Deb was away when Gotti needed to go to the eye doctor. I went over to the house to pick him up and first I had to call Deb to remind me which was Gucci and which was Gotti. They had just gotten their hair cut and looked like twins. One was running away from me, I should've known, it was Gotti. I picked him up, placed him half way in his traveling sack but had to stop and scratch my arm. The little dude jets away (who would want to be stuffed in that little bag) and I'm chasing him around the apartment. He knew I wasn't Deb and tried to push my limits! HA!

I finally pick him up AGAIN, got him half way in and he pushed out. We fought for about 10 minutes until I finally got him in there. He just looked at me like "Please get Mommy home!" We proceeded to the vet and ended up having quite a nice time. RIP little dude! xoxo

- Angela Mangone

Gotti was a special cat with a very wise and gentle soul. I'd come in to say hi and was always greeted by his silent "feed me now" meow. I was lucky enough to be there for many of his 9+ lives. I knew how much his mom loved him. I never knew how she would be able to handle "the" day, and I dreaded that for her. But I also knew he would want to make sure she was in good hands when he decided to go, and I'm pretty sure he and his brother Copper and sister Gucci had a discussion—this was his time & and it was okay.

Gotti's free now.

Thanks for being such a good guy Gott Gott. I feel grateful to have met your gentle soul.

- Julie Tomlinson aka "Aunt Julie"

19

BECOMING MASTER OF A HUMAN IS PAWSIBLE

Allyson was a professional dog walker. In fact, she was Chance and Parker's favorite dog walker. Several years before we met, she was living in an apartment on her own.

Her neighbor worked in real estate and went to clean out a house for sale. It was evident that the person who last lived in the house was a hoarder. They moved in a rush and left massive amounts of stuff behind, including two cats with food and water.

For at least two weeks, the cats were left to fend for themselves. The realtor took it upon herself to rescue them.

Knowing the kind, animal-loving heart of Allyson, she asked, "Would you like to foster these cats?"

"Yeah, I can do that." Allyson jumped to the task.

Both cats were sweet. One was also quite mischievous. Too mischievous. Little Girl was a free-spirit who could not be tied down to any single home. This rambunctious gal was constantly getting herself into high jinks. She became the community cat. All of the neighbors pitched in to feed her and give her affection.

The other cat, Coco, was very much an indoor cat. This gorgeous tortoiseshell girl was shy and low key, yet vocal. She was perfect company for easy-going Allyson.

Prior to becoming roommates, Allyson's friend, Jeremy, also took in a cat.

Neo was Jeremy's stunning black cat with a thin, yet distinguished patch of white on his chest. He was part of a litter of kittens that was found and rescued from a parking lot located on the grounds of Los Angeles Harbor College.

A friend of Jeremy's involved in cat rescue asked, "Would you like to adopt one of the litter, Jeremy? They are so adorable!"

"Sure, I'll take one."

Soon after adopting the young cat, Jeremy discovered Neo had asthma. Jeremy also discovered that Neo had a flair for dramatics. For a decade and counting, Jeremy has cared for his asthmatic cat. In return, Neo has kept Jeremy thoroughly entertained.

When Allyson and Jeremy decided to become roommates, they integrated their cats. Neo and Coco were not worst enemies, but also not besties. While tolerating each other from a distance, they both continued to hold their own title: Master of My Human. You'll hear more about these two felines in the next story.

20

FOSTERING IS PAWSIBLE

The month following Posey's (formerly known as Dolly) adoption, my heart moved me to foster for the first time. Yesenia, a dedicated South Los Angeles shelter worker, pleaded for help to save the life of Solobino. She was a spayed, brown and black, smooth-coated Chihuahua-Miniature Pinscher mix. This dainty girl was eight years old, and weighed only nine pounds.

Solobino's human did not have enough time to care for her, so she was surrendered to the shelter on September 26, 2013. As Thanksgiving neared, no one had shown any interest in this little girl.

I saw a few different social media posts seeking a kind, loving person to adopt or foster Solobino. Like so many I came across, I shared the posts in hopes that someone out there in cyberspace would step up.

Yesenia's heartache socked me in the gut when I read her final plea:

Solobino has been overlooked multiple times. I was finally able to take her out and she is the sweetest girl. She loves the attention. I couldn't believe someone that does independent "rescue" had said that Solobino would never get adopted or rescued and that she should be put down. She only met with Solobino for 5 minutes! Solobino came into the shelter scared and it took her a while to come out of her shell. She is still shy with strangers but once she feels comfortable with you she rolls over for belly rubs. Solobino came in with another dog and there is a memo that the owners said the dogs were fearful and may bite. Solobino's buddy was unfortunately not nice and as much as I tried to earn his trust he just did not improve as time passed by. Solobino has made great progress and the staff/volunteers that have taken her out have seen no aggression. She just needs someone that will go slow and give her time to get comfortable. She is on 24 hour alert and time is running out for her.

An incredibly giving, kind-hearted woman named Teri volunteered to fund Solobino's rescue. She was backed by a small, local rescue organization that had authority to pull dogs from the shelter. With a house full of her own adopted dogs, as well as a few fosters, this selfless woman was at capacity and couldn't foster Solobino herself. A foster was all that was needed to save this small dog's life.

It was my turn to step up.

I had no idea what was involved in being a foster mom to a shelter dog, but I knew that people who fostered were inspiring to me. They were superheroes. I had a hard time imagining myself opening my home and my heart to a down and out animal, only to say goodbye. I didn't think I could do it. Plus, didn't I need to be qualified? Take a test?

I turned to my friend, Jennifer, for guidance. She had a house full of dogs. At the time, she had four that she adopted. Last time I counted, she was up to five. She also constantly fostered one or two at a time.

"Jennifer, what do I need to do to become a dog foster parent?"

I was prepared to be let in on a secret and take detailed notes.

"Nothing. There's no training. No requirements."

"What? Really?"

"Really! You'll just fill out an application for whatever organization you are fostering for."

"What about expenses?"

"The rescue will cover any expenses incurred from your foster."

Well. Easy peasy. Done!

With the long Thanksgiving weekend coming up, I agreed to temporarily foster the little girl. My apartment building only allowed two dogs maximum, but I could get by with a nine pound dog "visiting" over a long holiday weekend.

With a lot of coordination efforts on Teri's part, Solobino was granted her freedom ride. One of the rescue organization's volunteers transported Solobino from the shelter to me.

A mix of excitement and uncertainty filled my insides as I waited on the steps outside my apartment building for the little doggy to arrive. I envisioned meeting a shy, fearful girl.

There they were! I started walking calmly toward them.

Solobino excitedly rushed toward me as the transporter held her leash and hurriedly walked behind her. All of my preconceived notions of this little girl were quickly wiped away.

"Hi! So nice to meet you. Thank you for bringing her to me."

"Thank you for fostering her! I'm so glad we were able to get her out of there."

"Me, too! She is nothing like I was expecting." The Chi-Min Pin mix clearly loved people and displayed her friendliness by standing on her hind legs and extending her front legs in the air, as if wanting a hug or to be picked up. I kneeled down to pet her.

"She's super sweet and friendly. Not at all aggressive as far as I have seen."

"I guess I will find out more when I introduce her to my dogs."

"Good luck! She's so happy to be out of that shelter. Thanks, again."

"My pleasure. Take care."

I walked along my neighborhood block with her for a bit to introduce Solobino to her new surroundings and empty her bladder. I was amazed by her outgoing, vivacious personality. Clearly, the shelter atmosphere was stressful to her, and she was elated to have her freedom back.

"Alright, little girl. Let's go meet Chance and Parker."

Since it was just me, I couldn't take the three dogs separately to meet on neutral ground, as is recommended for dog introductions. I decided to just go for it and bring the little girl straight into my apartment.

Knowing how my boys bombard me with hugs and affection when I open the door, I picked the little girl up and carried her as I walked into my apartment to avoid any chance of her getting trampled by two excited dogs.

As predicted, Chance and Parker came running to greet me at the door. They quickly noticed the surprise I had in my arms.

Parker belted out boisterous, yet enthusiastic barks that made Solobino nervous. She let out a tiny growl. I quickly corrected her, "Ssst. Ssst. You're okay."

Chance, my small dog protector, was gentle and curious.

I told my boys, "Back. Back. Sit! Stay."

"Good. Stay." I held out my hand in the stay command position they knew well. When they both reached a calm state, I put the small Chi-Min Pin mix down.

She approached them. Nose to nose sniffs. Nose to butt sniffs. Tails wagged. All good.

Wondering if she was house trained, I watched closely as she explored the apartment. My answer came fairly quickly. Uh oh. She peed on the living room carpet. We had some crate training to do.

Another to-do was a name change. "Solobino" just didn't do it for me. It was a long name that I wasn't even sure how to pronounce. Since I'm a wine lover and she looked like a delicate, dark grape, I named her Pinot.

One long holiday weekend turned into two. Two weekends turned into two weeks. Two weeks turned into two months.

Pinot fit right in with Chance and Parker. Chance had another little one to watch over. Pinot was his female mini-me. They looked identical with their sleek black coat and dark tan markings.

Parker gained a new playmate with whom he could race after balls. Pinot loved to play fetch with mini tennis balls. She also stole Parker's favorite napping spot on one of the back cushions of the couch.

Chance, Parker, and Pinot enjoyed daily adventures at the beach together. It was their favorite place and delivered quick smiles. As the trio's friendship grew, my bond with the little girl tightened. She was easy to love. When I was upset, she was the first to notice. She ran to my side and licked my tears. Sensitive, sensitive girl.

Pinot was a sleeping beauty. She had two favorite positions. Curled in a tight ball. Or, laid on her back with her little belly exposed and four thin legs stretched out as long and far as they could go. When morning delivered daylight, she placed her front paws over her eyes to block it out. "More sleep! More sleep!"

I continued networking Pinot for adoption. Many people we passed during walks stopped to inquire about my trio, "Are they all yours?"

"Well, two are. The little one is my foster. She's so sweet. If you know anyone looking to add a small dog to their family, she's available for adoption."

I met a couple prospective adopters this way, but my gut told me neither was right for her. Was I being too over-protective? Maybe. But, she deserved the best. Only the best would do.

Another bond that solidified as I fostered Pinot was the bond between her and my dog walker, Allyson. They adored each other!

Allyson and her roommate, Jeremy, expressed interest in adopting Pinot. They only had one concern. Well, two. Their cats.

It had been three years since they moved in together and introduced their cats, who respectfully tolerated each other's boundaries. When Allyson and Jeremy invited me to bring Pinot over to introduce her to their aloof cat and more aloof cat, we were all interested to see how it would go.

Pinot did well. She was curious. The cats? Let's just say, they valued their independence and space.

We all agreed it might be best not to add Pinot to the household mix. We wanted to alleviate any undue stress for the cats, as well as Allyson and Jeremy. I continued to foster Pinot. I also told my apartment manager about her.

"Hi, Donna*. You may have noticed I've been taking care of a third dog."

"Yes, I thought I saw you with another little dog."

"I'm fostering. It was only supposed to be for a weekend. That was two months ago. She's so quiet. Never barks. I can't believe nobody has adopted her yet."

"She is cute."

"Are you okay with me keeping her until I find her a home?"

"Just don't take her out when the building owners are here. They'll be around in a couple weeks. Two dogs is the max."

"I'll be careful. I'll be moving out within the next couple months anyway. I'll give you an exact date when I know."

*Name changed for privacy consideration.

"Okay. Sounds good."

As much as I loved Playa del Rey and my apartment, I had to move. I was struggling financially and needed to make some cuts to my budget.

In spring 2015, I found a cheap apartment that was three blocks from the dog beach in Long Beach. Everyone in the building had a dog. Some had two.

Before I moved in, I asked the apartment manager, "How many dogs are allowed? I have two of my own and am currently fostering a little 9-pound Min Pin mix."

"That's awesome! Everyone here loves dogs. I have one dog and foster all the time."

"So three will be okay?"

"Yeah, totally. The building owner is never here."

Perfect, I thought.

A month later, life looked good. Finances under control. Pinot and I were growing more and more attached. She got along splendidly with my boys. On Mother's Day, I accepted failure as a foster and decided to make her a permanent member of the family. I adopted her.

Although we moved out of Allyson's dog-walking territory, I coincidentally moved half a mile from her mother's house. Allyson's mom had Alzheimer's disease.

"Tes, would it be okay if I brought Pinot to visit my mom once or twice a week? I think it would perk her up."

"Absolutely! What a great idea. Let me know how she does."

After a few weeks of visits and getting acquainted, Allyson shared an update, "If Mom is in a sad mood, Pinot brings a smile to her face. When mom can't find the words, somehow Pinot brings them out of her."

Allyson's mom was just as much a gift to Pinot, whose face shined brightly in her new friend's arms. Pinot found her calling. She was an unofficial therapy dog.

Chance, Parker, Pinot, and I had a grand summer together. We became regulars at the dog beach, and I cherished the time spent with these three seniors.

Unfortunately, fall delivered stormy weather.

The first zapped me via telephone. I received a call from the owner of the apartment building I moved into just over six months prior. He spoke to me in a condescending tone.

"So, Tes. I saw you walking the other morning. You had three dogs with you. Are all three of those dogs yours?"

I thought about lying. I couldn't.

"Yes," I replied.

"Your lease is clear. You cannot have three dogs living in that apartment. The idea is ridiculous. Having more than one dog is a privilege meant for home owners. You have one dog on your lease and one dog can live there. You are breaking your lease. If the other two are not out immediately, you will be evicted."

"I am happy to give you an additional deposit or increased rent. They are all seniors. They are quiet and well-behaved."

"No. That is too many dogs for that apartment."

It was a one bedroom apartment with a patio. If I had three 80-pound dogs, he might have a point. Mine were 38-pounds, 20 pounds and 9 pounds. They all got plenty of exercise with at least three walks a day and a minimum of four outings to the dog beach each week.

"May I propose that I keep two and you can increase my rent?"

"I will discuss it with my business partner and get back to you."

He got back to me within 24 hours with an emphatic, "No!" and again threatened to evict me. I had three days to come up with a solution.

It's hard enough to find affordable rental living quarters that allow one dog, let alone two. Three dogs? Unheard of. It didn't matter that all three of my dogs were seniors, well-behaved, and got more exercise than many dogs who live in a home with a yard.

I was in tears. My brain immediately went into problem solving mode. I had to do whatever I could to keep all my dogs safe. I would not allow any of them to step foot in a shelter.

Chance needed to stay with me because he required the most care. At 11 years old, he started experiencing some mysterious neurological issues for which he was receiving treatment from a holistic veterinarian.

For Parker's care, I turned to my mom. Parker loved her and my stepdad. They generously agreed to watch him for five months until my lease was up and I could move out.

My heart was devastated for Parker and Chance. They were bonded. Parker was sure to think we abandoned him. Chance was likely to fall into a depression. At least they would be safe, cared for, and loved.

I called Allyson to let her know what was going on. With incredible compassion, she offered to care for Pinot until my lease was up. I was speechless. And, incredibly grateful. There was no one better to care for her.

I wasn't the only person in the building that was confronted about multiple dogs. A couple with two dogs was also threatened to be evicted. They arranged for a friend to watch their second dog, a Staffordshire Terrier, for two weeks while they obtained a medical letter from their therapist stating that the dog was an emotional support animal.

The Fair Housing Amendments Act of 1988, Section 504 of the Rehabilitation Act of 1973, and Title II of the Americans with Disabilities Act protect the right of people with disabilities to keep emotional support animals. Even landlords with explicit no-pet policies are legally obligated to allow emotional therapy dogs to live with their human.

I could have done the same thing, I suppose. All three were truly my emotional support system in my battle against chronic depression. I didn't want to stir the pot and put the other tenants' legitimate claim in jeopardy. I was grateful my dogs were all safe in the hands of loving, kind people. It sucked, but so many people out there face similar plights without friends or family to turn to for help. I was fortunate. It was going to be okay.

Chance and I visited Parker two and half hours away in Bakersfield as often as we could. As for Pinot, even though she was nearby, we kept visits to a minimum. She had experienced so much upheaval over the last year, we didn't want to confuse her.

Allyson and Jeremy re-introduced Pinot to the cats with a new strategy. They put up a gate to limit Pinot's apartment access to part of the living room and dining area. Both Neo and Coco had free range of the apartment with their stealth-like jumping abilities. Within two days, everyone found their groove and felt comfortable living under the same roof.

I checked in with Allyson every few weeks to make sure Pinot was fitting in well, "Hey, Allyson! How are things going?"

"Things are good. Pinot is doing well. She's really happy."

"Oh, that's so great. I cannot tell you how glad I am to hear that. She's getting along with the cats?"

"She tends to get along with Neo a little better than Coco. Coco is shy and likes to hang in my room. Sometimes, Pinot will jump onto my bed with a blind landing. Guess who is usually right there?"

"Uh-oh. Coco?"

"Yeah. Pinot freaks her out when she does that. Other than that, they get along okay."

"Oh, good. I'm glad she isn't creating a stressful living environment."

"No, no. She's doing well. She's taken on some kitty habits. She sleeps and cleans herself like a cat now."

"Oh, my gosh. That's funny."

"Yeah, she's really cute."

As weeks and months passed, Pinot found contentment in Allyson and Jeremy's care. She charmed them with her silly mannerisms and tender heart. Allyson continued to bring her on visits to see her mom to offer cheer and comfort.

As March 31, the end of my lease, drew near, Allyson and I discussed the possibility of her and Jeremy adopting Pinot.

"Do you really want to adopt her?"

"Yes, if that would be okay with you. I love her. Jeremy adores her. He's been going through a tough time, and she's been there for him. She's offered him so much emotional support."

"I can relate to that. She is an extremely sensitive, compassionate girl."

I felt like the three of them were meant to be together all along.

Sincerity poured from my heart, "I cannot think of a better match for Pinot than the two of you. I would love for you guys to adopt her!"

Pinot's life is filled with adventure and comfort. When she's not taking a nap, she is enjoying afternoon and weekend getaways in beach cities along the southern California coast. One of her favorite things to do is hang with Jeremy and Allyson at outdoor cafes.

Pinot is a small dog who offers the enormous gift of emotional healing to those she meets. I am grateful that Yesenia recognized her potential for greatness at the shelter and worked so hard to get her out. I am grateful for the joy-filled eleven months Pinot shared with Chance, Parker, and me. Most of all, I am grateful that Pinot found her perfect happy ending with Jeremy, Allyson, and two feline friends.

As for Chance, Parker, and me, the three of us got our happy ending, too. We were reunited and gratefully living under one roof together again.

RABBITS HAVE PAWS, TOO

21-1

CREATING A BUNNY SANCTUARY IS PAWSIBLE

Let's face it. Rabbits are cute. Their big, floppy ears bring on smiles and wonderment. Their adorable, twitching noses induce giggles. Their silky fur can make a petting hand feel as if it is melting with each gentle caress.

Along with the cuteness factor, comes the care factor. Rabbits are a big responsibility. They require special attention and special housing to keep them safe and feel secure. Often people get excited about adding a bunny to their family—especially around Easter time. Unfortunately, it is not rare for that initial excitement to fade. Families get busy with activities and their pet bunny becomes an afterthought rather than a priority. For this reason combined with other people reasons, like moving, rabbits are the third most-surrendered pet to shelters, after cats and dogs.

While many people view rabbits as pets, they are also viewed as a commodity. Some people, including many homesteaders, breed, raise, and process rabbits just for their meat. In recent years, rabbits have been reintroduced to restaurant menus, as well as food markets and grocery stores, as an exotic meat. In addition to being killed for their meat, rabbits can also be killed for their fur. They are not strangers to product testing, either. Rabbits are often victims of the testing of razor blades, as well as toxic chemicals for a variety of industries, including cosmetics and transportation.

Some bunnies are fortunate enough to escape such horrible fates. The magical world of rabbit rescue holds the truth that anything is possible. It is a world filled with selfless heroes who save and nurture down-and-out rabbits, making their impossible bunny dreams come true.

Naomi is a champion of rabbits. She calls herself a Devoted Rabbit Slave at Bunny Farm Sanctuary. Her home is not an official sanctuary, but rather a permanent resort-like home for the rabbits who are fortunate enough to find themselves in her care. Naomi's bunnies are some of the luckiest bunnies in the world.

Naomi has always had a love for animals, especially rabbits, which have been part of her life for 25 years. As a teenager, she had a few pet rabbits. The first rabbit she rescued and cared for with great devotion entered her life nearly twenty years ago when she was a young adult. Chewie was rescued by a woman who found him in the mouth of a dog at a horse stable. After he lived with that woman for 18 months, Naomi rescued Chewie from her. He was receiving inadequate care.

Naomi provided Chewie with a safe living environment, fed him a healthy diet, and got him neutered. She joined Etherbun, a Yahoo group forum, where she exchanged tips with other rabbit-loving people about proper rabbit care.

Chewie opened Naomi's eyes to the world of rabbits from a new point of view. She learned how misunderstood they are. Bunnies are not easy pets. Placing them in a hutch and remembering them only at feeding time is unkind care. They are smart, mischievous, sociable, and sensitive animals. They need room to roam and explore—to exercise their body and mind.

Chewie fueled Naomi's passion for these precious creatures. She decided to dedicate her life to rescuing rabbits. According to Naomi, people have to earn a rabbit's trust and respect. Naomi enjoys the challenge of winning a rabbit's love. Since Chewie, twenty rabbits have become masters of her household.

21-2

SAVING SHOW RABBITS IS PAWSIBLE

Belle, Hannah, and Jack were retiring show rabbits. Like countless other show rabbits, they were forced into retirement because they were not good enough. All three no longer met standards set by rabbit breeders and were fated for the chopping block. One moment, they were being admired for their beauty. The next, they were at a meat auction where they were to be bid on to be someone's next meal. How did it come to this?

Belle was a winning show rabbit. She started winning shows when she was only six months old. Her owners wanted to keep her high-quality bloodline going, so they turned her into a breeding rabbit by the time she was ten months old. They bred Belle twice. In her breeders' eyes, she failed because she was not able to produce enough kits. They had expectations of her producing 6 – 8 winning show bunnies for them. She could only produce four or less. Now, useless to them, they sent her on a truck to a meat auction.

Hannah never made it as a show rabbit. Her very minor flaws meant that she was just not good enough. Her blaze, which is an even wedge of white that runs up a rabbit's face, was a little bit too wide for a black and white Dutch. Her coloring and other markings didn't meet show quality standards either. Being imperfect meant being sold for food. She was loaded on a truck headed to the same meat auction as Belle.

Jack also came up short in meeting show quality standards. He, too, had coloring and markings that weren't quite up to snuff. Beyond that, he was too tiny, weighing a mere 2 ½ pounds. His destiny was a truck bound to the exact same meat auction as Belle and Hannah.

These three rabbits, along with thousands of others, were doomed to meet their death. Death for these "retired" show bunnies—or any auction bunnies, for that matter—is not kind. It is not peaceful. Instead, it is utterly cruel.

WARNING: THE FOLLOWING SECTION CONTAINS GRAPHIC DESCRIPTIONS OF THE TORTUROUS TREATMENT OF INNOCENT ANIMALS.

Oftentimes, two- or three-day-old babies are killed by slamming their precious heads against a hard countertop, rendering them unconscious. Their limp, helpless bodies are then tossed in a freezer to "finish them off." Of all common killing practices, this is considered to be the most humane.

Another common practice is slitting rabbits' throats.

One of the more horrific ways that rabbits are killed for their meat is sticking them in large, closed containers, and then pumping carbon monoxide inside with a tube. The rabbits suffocate and experience a slow, arduous, terrifying death.

In the case of Hannah, market breeders were going to take a hammer and smash her skull.

THE GRAPHIC DESCRIPTIONS OF TORTUROUS TREATMENT OF INNOCENT ANIMALS ARE OVER.

Wise to these cruel, yet common, practices, a hero stepped up to the plate. A gentleman attended the auction where Belle, Hannah, and Jack had been delivered. He purchased as many rabbits as he could fit into his truck and then called his friend at East Valley Bunny Rescue as soon as all the rabbits were loaded safely.

"I just bought a truck full of beautiful rabbits. I couldn't stand to see them being sold for meat. Can you help me out? Can you take them?"

"Bless you! How many do you have?"

"Close to two dozen."

"I can take most of them. We'll figure out good situations for the rest."

Shortly after the bunnies arrived, Sue, the shelter owner, sent an email to Naomi, who had previously adopted from her. Sue knew how much Naomi loved rabbits and how well she cared for them.

"They're so smart, sassy, and independent. Such incredible little beings!" Naomi once excitedly professed her soft spot for Dutches to the bunny rescuer.

Rescuers take a chance adopting beloved animals out. They can do background checks, but there are no guarantees of the quality of life the animals will have. The bunny rescuer at East Valley Bunny Rescue knew that with Naomi, any rabbit she adopted would get a high quality life. Naomi dedicated her life to them. Besides that, anyone willing to drive 16 hours round trip through the California desert to Mesa, Arizona, is truly devoted. Naomi had made that trip five times.

Pictures of Belle, Hannah, and Jack were enough to make Naomi's heart melt. Initially, she was only going to adopt Belle and Jack, but Hannah tug-tug-tugged at Naomi's heartstrings. And, so did the bunny rescuer, "Hannah is such a special little girl. I know of all people, Naomi, you could give her the lovely life she deserves."

Naomi couldn't leave Hannah behind. She decided to adopt all three.

21-3

BONDING WITH A BUNNY IS PAWSIBLE

It wasn't just three rabbits that Naomi brought home with her the day she met Belle, Hannah, and Jack. While at the East Valley Bunny Rescue, a fourth rabbit caught Naomi's eye.

"Oh, Sue. This girl is a beauty! How did she end up here?"

"Isn't she gorgeous? Her name is Marri. Poor thing. I got a call from a good Samaritan. Only three months old and she was found tied to a light pole on the I-10 freeway in Phoenix. We went out right away to get her."

"Thank goodness you did. The world is both cruel and kind."

"It certainly is. Some of the horrific things we see …," her voice trailed off as she recalled past rescues; then she returned to the present. "She did get adopted, but they returned her within 24 hours. Maybe she's meant for you, Naomi?"

Without hesitation, Naomi agreed, "Yes, I adore her! Do you think she would make a good mate for Jack?"

"You could keep them in the same crate on the drive home to bond them. Have you ever heard of bonding by stress? A long car ride home is ideal for this bonding method," Sue suggested.

"Yes, I've heard of it. The sound of the engine and the movement of the vehicle is just stressful enough to distract them from fighting."

"Exactly. I'm sorry I haven't had a chance to introduce them prior. We just have too many animals here."

"It's fine. I will ride in the back seat with them to supervise the entire eight hour ride. We will also take a few 30-minute breaks."

"That should work well," Sue was confident these rabbits were in excellent hands.

"They look so attractive together with the same brown coloring. Of course, we both know that it's all up to them. They decide whether to bond or not!" Naomi laughed.

"You got that right," Sue agreed.

The women loaded up the four bunnies into Naomi's vehicle. Belle and Hannah each had their own crate, while Jack and Marri shared one in an attempt to create a bonded pair. Naomi sat in the back seat with them as her husband drove.

After an eight-hour-drive home, Naomi released all four of the bunnies in a safe, neutral territory just to see what would happen and how they would interact.

Much to Naomi's surprise, Marri determined that she had strong feelings of dislike for both Jack and Hannah within 30 minutes. In fact, the feisty girl tried to beat both of them up! As a result, Jack and Hannah bonded immediately. It was love at first sight.

Instead of Jack, Marri selected Naomi as her mate. She adored her human and happily went wherever Naomi went. She became a great little traveler and accompanied Naomi on road trips to see Naomi's mom. Every time Naomi packed, she was sure to include Marri's hideaway hopper.

"Oh, Marri! You have more luggage than I do!"

Each visit, Marri is treated like the special, much-loved guest that she is—even getting her own room.

Some rabbits like and prefer the company of humans. Marri is one of those rabbits.

21-4

A GENIUS BUNNY IS PAWSIBLE

Not all rabbits bond with a mate. Such is the case with Belle. Even so, she does graciously share her living space with Chase. Each has their own hideaway hopper so they can maintain their own personal space. Like Marri, Chase is one of those rabbits who really likes to be around humans. He adores his Naomi.

Chase is a black and white Dutch rabbit who was found wandering around a neighborhood in Scottsdale, Arizona. He was less than six months old and fortunate enough to be turned in to the hands of East Valley Bunny Rescue.

Chase was taken to an adoption event at a local PetSmart®. Naomi's friend, Kim, was volunteering at the event and was blown away by Chase's intelligence. With 25 years of experience raising and caring for rabbits, Kim knows her stuff. She knew this amazing creature needed an exceptional human to care for him. Naomi came to mind, and she reached for her phone.

"Hi, Naomi! It's Kim. Guess where I am and who I'm with?"

"Kim, hi! Let me see. It must have something to do with rabbits?" She chuckled.

"You got it. I'm at an adoption event. You have to see this rabbit. His name is Chase, and he's highly intelligent, inquisitive, and just a ball full of energy. He really needs to live with an experienced rabbit person. Of course, I thought of you! Can I send you some photos and videos?"

"He sounds incredible. Yes, please, send away."

Naomi fell in love with him instantly. She knew she could provide this practically human rabbit with the home he needed and deserved. She repeated the same long trek to Arizona that she made when she adopted Belle, Hannah, Jack, and Marri. Only this time it was during the high desert heat of July. He was worth it!

Naomi calls Chase the "King of Everything." His personality is large. His charm is magnetizing. Chase's inquisitive nature far surpasses that of the average rabbit. Watching him is like watching a mischievous toddler. Naomi keeps at least one eye on him at all times, deterring him from getting into things he should not. If he doesn't get his way, Chase has been known to throw a child-like tantrum. When he does get his way, he is happy as can be.

While most rabbits proceed with curious caution when they encounter an open door, Chase sees it as an invitation to investigate what is on the other side. From room doors and closet doors to cabinets and suitcases—if it opens and shuts, Chase is there to inspect and explore.

Naomi and her family do their best to ensure that anything that can be opened is properly shut. If a door is ajar or a gate is improperly closed or blocked, Chase puts on his clever engineering hat. He takes great glee in assessing how to get up, over, under, or around any obstacles that lie before him, then makes a calculated, quick escape to the other side.

Chase is also bright enough to know how good he has it in Naomi's care at Bunny Farm Sanctuary, so he never goes too far. He finds satisfaction in solving the mystery of the escape but has no interest in far-off adventures.

His curiosity and smarts also make Chase an excellent detective. When a fancy dumbo eared rat found refuge in Naomi's carport one winter, she enlisted Chase to help rescue her. Naomi caught glimpses of the adorable brown rat and was sure she had been someone's pet at some point. She named her Emma.

For five long, cold months Emma lived in some old blankets under Naomi's carport, which was 70-feet long and 20-feet wide. Along with a car, the carport was packed full of boxes and other storage containers. Countless hiding spots were at little Emma's disposal. When temperatures were warm enough for Chase to endure, he and Naomi started their search and rescue. Chase's job was to find. Naomi's job was to capture.

"Chase, go find the rat. Go find Emma," Naomi said.

With great determination and dedication to the task at hand, Chase used his keen nose and ears to track down Emma. Once he picked up her scent and zoned in on her, he used his ears to alert Naomi and point her in Emma's direction. Quietly he eased his way toward Emma. When he reached her, he sat in front of her and didn't move.

It took Naomi several attempts to capture Emma, but Chase's detective work was accurate every single time. Naomi was awestruck by his incredible feat. Emma was grateful. She now had a warm, safe, loving home.

Along with his high intelligence, Chase is also personable, caring, and outgoing. He loves all humans and all rabbits. He enjoys visiting Club Med, which is a climate-controlled room where Naomi's elder, disabled bunnies live and are provided with special love and care.

Chase is quite a few years younger than the elders. He delivers joy to his seniors much like a baby brings joy to elderly people living in a retirement home. Although he is not bonded with any of the senior bunnies, he is extremely gentle with them. His nose wiggles in delight as he sniffs their toes and chins. The elder rabbits trust him and enjoy his visits, which are always supervised and fun for Naomi to watch.

Chase is a genius bunny that finds fulfillment in solving problems, actively playing detective, and practicing compassion. After a hard day's work, he gets plenty of good rest. Chase loves to get up on the second floor of his two-story hide-away condo to take a long nap every afternoon. Ah! The life of a rabbit at Naomi's Bunny Farm Sanctuary. Paradise!

21-5

FOSTER FAILING IS PAWSIBLE

Just like dogs and cats, rabbits can end up in the animal shelter system. Sometimes they are strays. Sometimes, owner surrenders. Unfortunately, most shelters are not equipped to care for rabbits long term.

Ricky and Lucy, a bonded pair, were in a Los Angeles county shelter that happened to work with a local rabbit rescue. Volunteers for the rescue would come in to care for the rabbits and do their best to get them out of the shelter as fast as possible. Ricky's time was up at the shelter. Since Lucy was his bonded mate, she would be euthanized with him.

Try as they might, the rescue could not find any local housing or boarding in the Los Angeles area for the sweet fuzzy duo. Determined to save their lives, volunteers scrambled and reached out to every rabbit-loving person they knew within and beyond the City of Angels. Everyone sighed in relief and cheered with gratitude when a volunteer's family member located in Bishop, California, kindly offered to provide the pair a foster home. They were welcome to stay as long as needed. She had a three-feet by five-feet outdoor garden pen for them to call home, whether temporary or permanent.

To get them safely to their new digs, travel arrangements were made with a rabbit transit organization called The Bunderground Railroad. Rabbit loving people who lived along the route from Los Angeles to Bishop signed up for different legs of the trip. Thanks to amazing, selfless volunteers, Ricky and Lucy's freedom ride was set!

One of those transportation volunteers was Naomi. For her leg of the transport, she drove 90 miles north of her home to pick up Ricky and Lucy. She also volunteered to be their temporary foster for a month until their permanent foster home was ready.

For 30 days, Naomi cared for and got to know Ricky and Lucy. When the time arrived to take them to their long-term foster, Naomi couldn't do it. The idea of saying goodbye broke her heart. She called the rescue and confessed, "I am a lousy transporter and a lousy foster. I cannot bring myself to say goodbye. I have fallen in love."

"There are worse things to fail at!" The rescuer was smiling on the other end of the phone.

"They have been living in great comfort at my house. They have their own room with their own bunny condo. The idea of them living out their lives in a small garden pen on a patio where summer temps are over 90 degrees and down into the 20s during wintertime. I just can't bear the idea."

"Would you like to adopt them?"

"I would." And, she did.

21-6

A SURPRISE IS PAWSIBLE

Jordan, a baby blue-eyed Dutch bunny, was found wandering the streets of Mesa, Arizona. Younger than five months, she was picked up by animal control and taken to East Valley Bunny Rescue. Shortly after arriving at the rescue, Jordan gave her new human friends a big surprise. She delivered five kits–four boys and a girl. Nobody at the rescue had any idea she was pregnant.

When the kits were old enough, three of the boys were separated from their mom and placed in a hutch of their own. The girl and the fourth boy stayed in a hutch with their momma.

Knowing Naomi's extreme affection for blue-eyed Dutches, which are quite rare, one of the rescue's volunteers called her, "Naomi, these Dutches are exquisite. I'll send you some pictures and videos."

Naomi fell in love with the momma rabbit and her babies instantly. She called her friend back, "I adore them and would like to adopt all three."

"I knew you would!"

"My only challenge is that I cannot drive down to Arizona right now. But I'm going to contact The Bunderground Railroad and see if they can transport."

"I'm sure they will help you find a way. Thank you so much for adopting these three. You will give them a lovely, happy life. I'm so excited for them!"

Naomi reached out to Christine, a member of The Bunderground Railroad. When she's not working, Christine often travels all over California, Arizona, and Nevada, transporting rabbits.

"Yes, I can do it. Happy to! I have a few days off later in the week, so it's perfect timing." This selfless woman picked up the precious cargo in Arizona and then transported them to Naomi in California. Seeing Naomi's face light up with pure joy when she saw the thumping trio nuzzled together sweetly in their carrier was Christine's reward.

Naomi had a special room set up for her new family members, Jordan, Rosie, and Macey. On the bunnies' first night in their forever home, Naomi placed the carrier on the floor of their room. She gently opened the carrier door and then quietly backed out of the room. She sat and watched the trio peacefully from a place where they couldn't spot her. One by one they cautiously popped out of the carrier, ran a lap around the room, thumped, and ran back inside where they felt safe.

Since the bunnies were born in a shelter and had experienced little human attention or contact up to this point, they were extremely timid in their new home. In fact, they were quite terrified. Having a wise understanding of the rabbit mind, along with a compassionate heart, Naomi let the three explore or hide at their own free will.

There was a futon bed in their room that offered many hiding places for Jordan, Rosie, and Macey during the first weeks in their new home. When Naomi put food out, they would wait until she left—after it was quiet and dark—and then slowly creep out from their hiding spots to enjoy their meal. Naomi continued to hide to watch them. Her face beamed with pride and joy as she witnessed their confidence grow. Each day they came out of their shells a tiny bit more.

After three months, Jordan, Rosie, and Macey were finally acclimated to humanity. Well, at least to Naomi. Gone were the days when they would cautiously sneak out of their carrier or hiding spot and then zip back inside. Instead, they started dancing around Naomi's feet at the sight of her. Naomi's heart fluttered with joy as she joined them.

Naomi likes the underdog, and rabbits are underdogs. They are often misunderstood, but when you get to know them, they are precious little beings. To earn a rabbit's trust is the highest honor. Humans have to work hard to gain their trust and receive their love. For Naomi that is the biggest reward—for them to show her they love her, show her they are happy.

Just watching rabbits play and hang out makes Naomi laugh. Anytime she's struggling or having a hard time, all she has to do is watch them romp around, and she can't help but smile. These funny, smart, silly beings always cheer her up.

You can support the efforts of Naomi and other rabbit rescuers by using cruel-free products. Check out the website, www.leapingbunny.org. It lists companies that are cruel-free to bunnies. All of them are audited. In order to maintain their listing and membership, the companies must meet standards from the beginning of their manufacturing all the way to the end of it.

Also, read product labels carefully. "This finished product not tested on animals" is a tricky statement. It is possible that the product is completely cruel-free. It is also possible that some of the ingredients within the making of the product have been tested on animals.

If you would like to adopt a bunny, there are rescues all across the country that will help you find the perfect match for you. House Rabbit Society, www.rabbit.org, has a website that offers great resources for rabbit care, local veterinary listings, rescue, and more.

The world needs more people like Naomi—people who are committed to providing rabbits with great love and devotion for their entire lifetime. Maybe that's you?

22

MAKING ANIMALS A PRIORITY IN YOUR COMMUNITY IS PAWSIBLE

In 2012, Sandy worked at an elementary school in Bakersfield, California, located in a low-income neighborhood next to a large park. To this day, people who live in the area tend not to spay or neuter their animals. As a result, unwanted litters of puppies are repeatedly dumped in the park.

The dogs run around loose in the area in packs. At one point in time, the strays were so prevalent that school staff had to take shifts guarding the gates to prevent dogs in search of shelter from entering the school. Kern County Animal Control regularly made rounds in the neighborhood. At times, they would set up crates in the park to trap the dogs, taking in four dogs every single day from this one area. Every single day. That's 28 dogs a week. From just one park in a large city filled with nearly 60 parks.

Those numbers add up. Especially, considering the low adoption rates of Kern county.

As you might imagine, the county shelter in Bakersfield was extremely overcrowded. Combined with the six other Kern county shelters facing similar challenges, the euthanize rates were tragically and unnecessarily high.

The average percentage of adoptable animals euthanized in shelters across the United States is approximately 50 percent. Kern County shelters were at an astronomical 64 percent in 2011, as reported by The Bakersfield Californian. That translates to 19,776 home-worthy dogs and cats killed.

With the sad statistics in mind, Sandy and her co-workers did their best to help as many homeless dogs as they could, but it was and continues to be an overwhelming problem. A problem that everyone at the school agreed could best be solved if the county handed out spay and neuter vouchers to local residents.

Knowing that Sandy was on the lookout for a Dachshund to add to her family, her co-worker approached, "Sandy, there are a few puppies out there. One of them is a Dachshund. I saw the animal control vehicle coming this way to get them."

Sandy rushed out the door. She ran toward the Animal Control employee as he put two young dogs in his transport vehicle. When she reached him, he was scooping up the little Dachshund puppy.

"Hi there!" Sandy greeted the gentleman.

"Hi!"

"How old do you think that one is?"

"About five weeks, I would say."

"What are they going to do with him when you bring him to the pound?" Sandy asked.

"They'll put him to sleep. He has an open wound." He pointed to a gash on his upper back near his shoulder blade.

"Oh, no. No, please give him to me. I'll take him."

"Well, I'm not supposed to give him to you because he has an open wound."

"I'll take him to the vet today."

"You'll take him to the vet?"

"Yes, I'll bring him into the school right now and when I get off work, I'll take him directly to the vet."

He hesitated for a moment, then replied, "Okay."

Sympathetic to her desire to help, he handed the little one over to Sandy.

In addition to the open wound, the wee one was infested with fleas. Sandy found a small box and padded it with a towel. She put the little guy she named Rex in the uncovered box and made sure he was cozy. She brought Rex home to bathe and feed him. Shortly after, they went to the vet to tend to that open wound and get him up to date on shots.

Rex had a lucky day. Instead of facing a sure-fire death sentence like thousands of puppies born and dumped in Bakersfield, he was welcomed into a loving family of five humans and a Lhasa Apso sister named Lanie.

About a year later, Sandy considered adopting another dog. Lanie was a senior and had some health issues. Sandy wanted to make sure Rex had a companion and would not be a single dog.

The timing just happened to be two weeks prior to a bitter split between the city and county animal shelters who were in dispute cost-sharing. The City of Bakersfield Animal Care Center and Kern County Animal Control shared a facility. The city owned the facility, while the county leased. The city chose not to renew the lease when it expired on September 30, 2013, and evicted the county animal control.

The separation set off a social media frenzy. Rumors spread like wildfire that more than 700 animals would be euthanized if they were not adopted before the county animal shelter moved to a new facility.

A spokesperson for the county facility dispelled the rumors and encouraged people to come adopt. In an effort to transport as few animals as possible, Kern County Animal Control dropped adoption fees for dogs to $15 and adoption fees for cats to $5.

The incentive—combined with all the horrific rumors—worked. The public came to the rescue by adopting 329 shelter animals over a two week period. Many rescue organizations, near and far also helped by welcoming more than 200 of the animals into their care.

The combined efforts reduced the population of pets the county had to transport to 280 dogs and cats. Quite a feat for a shelter with a daily population that hovered around 750 animals.

Sandy decided to go to the shelter in the midst of this storm to find a companion for Rex. She met a friendly Papillon mix who would make a perfect BFF (best friend forever) for skittish Rex. She put her name in to adopt him. A few days later, after his hold period expired, Sandy and her husband, Greg, returned to bring him home. During those few days of waiting, he became seriously ill.

The shelter had him on antibiotics and told the couple, "Sorry, but you will need to wait ten more days. He needs to get better before we can release him."

Highly concerned for this little one, Sandy went back every day to check on him. Every day he was worse. At one point, he didn't look like he was going to make it.

After an agonizing wait, Sandy was able to bring him home. His health was still poor. She immediately took him to the veterinarian.

"Sandy, you got this one out with little time to spare. He is really, really sick."

"What is wrong with him? Will he get better?"

"He has an upper respiratory infection. I'm going to prescribe some different antibiotics than what the shelter had him on. He also has kennel cough, so keep him away from your other animals."

As hard as she tried to keep the ailing Papillon separated from her other two dogs, they both caught kennel cough, too. With dedicated care and lots of love, Sandy and her family nursed the new pup they named Little Guy back to full health. They also rid the rest of the pack of kennel cough.

Rex and Little Guy quickly became the best of friends. Little Guy's friendly, laid back demeanor helped relax a more high-strung Rex. Lanie preferred to sit back and watch the two play. Her admiring eyes often grew droopy and took her to Napland.

In May 2014, Greg, who worked at another Bakersfield school, got a surprise upon his arrival to work one day. He called Sandy as she was headed out of town, "Honey, guess what was sitting outside the doorstep at school today?"

"Oh, no. What?"

"A box of one-week old kittens." He sent her a photo of three yellow and two calico kittens.

Even though the euthanasia rate at the city and county shelters was declining, it was still high. Sandy urged her husband, "Oh, gosh. Don't take them to the pound. Chances of them getting adopted are low. They will probably be put to sleep. Go get them some kitten milk and bottles. When I get back, we'll figure something out."

One of Greg's co-workers was infamous for her love of cats. She had ten under her care. With the understanding that she wasn't keeping any of the kittens from this abandoned litter, she offered to temporarily care for them.

A month went by and the woman who took all five kittens under her wing approached Greg and another co-worker at school, "The kittens are adorable, but I'm leaving on vacation soon. Somebody needs to take them. One was adopted, but there are still four left."

Greg and Sandy arrived at the woman's house that evening to check out the kittens. Greg's co-worker was there getting acquainted with the cats, too.

They were all overwhelmed by the idea of taking in four cats.

Sandy looked at their friend and suggested, "If you take two, we'll take two."

"Deal!"

Sandy and Greg's kids named the female Sassy. The male, Toby, took a quick liking to the family's rabbit, Buttercup. The two amuse themselves by playing tag together in the grass. All three live in peace and harmony with their canine companions, Lanie, Rex, and Little Guy.

As for Bakersfield and Kern County, the split between the shelters proved to be a benefit for the local animals. The flare-up between the two ignited awareness in the area about the importance of adoption, as well as spaying and neutering pets. Although euthanasia rates are still high, they are on a declining trend.

Those rates are expected to continue to decline thanks to the allocation of $250,000 toward spay and neuter programs approved by the Kern County Board of Supervisors for the fiscal year 2015/2016 budget.

Also making a positive impact in the community are exceptional dog rescue organizations.

Marley's Mutts Dog Rescue, a non-profit organization, rescues, rehabilitates, trains, and re-homes death row dogs from Kern County's high-kill animal shelters.

No Kill Kern is a rescue organization on the move to end euthanasia in all Kern County shelters. It is a Whole Earth Pets Foundation, Inc. program, which is a charity organization that supports programs and education to keep pets with their families.

With community awareness and involvement, the City of Bakersfield and Kern County are changing for the good of the people and betterment of the animals.

23

BEING A HERO IS PAWSIBLE

It is my greatest hope that the stories of rescue and adoption shared within this book inspire all who read them to responsibly adopt an animal in need of a forever, loving home. Adopting is an act of heroism. To adopt an animal is to save a life.

During the course of writing *Anything Is PAWSible*, I had the opportunity to meet and become part of an incredibly compassionate community. I had the opportunity to meet and speak with countless heroes.

Everyone who shared their story with me and allowed me to include it in this book is a hero.

Shelter workers and volunteers are heroes. They provide care, love, and affection to scared animals that wind up in a shelter by no fault of their own. The only hope for these animals is to be adopted by a loving family or individual. Shelter workers and volunteers get to know these animals and begin the networking process to find them homes. Unless it is a no-kill shelter, most dogs, cats, rabbits, and turtles will not get out alive, especially if they are seniors, sick, or injured. For the worthy animals that do not escape the confines of a shelter, these amazing people provide them with their last experience on earth. Their heroic work makes the last living moment for hundreds of thousands of animals a loving, compassionate one.

People who network animals are heroes. They work hard to get animals out of the shelter by taking photographs of adoptable animals and posting them on social media. Sharing these posts is an act of heroism. The combined efforts of people posting and sharing animals available for adoption over social media and email are proven to increase the chances of saving their lives.

Anyone involved with an animal rescue organization is a hero. From the founders to volunteers, these wonderful individuals bend over backwards and work around the clock to save animals from the streets, pull them out of shelters, rehabilitate and train them, and find loving and forever homes for them. It's an emotional roller coaster ride. Somehow, they manage to persevere. They are unstoppable.

Careful and mindful transporters and transportation coordinators are heroes. Whether driving or flying across the country, these remarkable individuals carry a heavy weight of responsibility on their shoulders. Some dogs and cats are en route to foster families. Others are headed to their new forever homes. All have been granted a second chance and a fresh start. Transporters and transportation coordinators ensure that saved animals travel in comfort with minimal stress and arrive at their destination safely.

People who foster animals are heroes. Not only do they provide a safe haven for animals and help them find their new, forever homes, but they also free up more space for other down and out animals in shelters, and enable rescue organizations to save more lives. The more fosters who volunteer for shelters and rescues, the more animals that shelters and rescues can save.

People who make donations are heroes. Whether you contribute funds to your favorite rescue group or to the care of a specific rescued animal, financial support is vital to saving lives.

People and organizations that create and implement innovative programs to assist both animals and the people who love them are heroes. One of my favorites, Shelter Intervention Program, was implemented by Downtown Dog Rescue (DDR) in Los Angeles. Since April 2013, volunteer counselors have helped prevent thousands of animals from entering the Los Angeles animal shelter system by educating and assisting people who thought surrendering their pet to a shelter was their only option. DDR continuously reminds the community, "We all need a little help sometimes." Lori Weise, the founder of DDR, recently wrote the book, *First Home, Forever Home*, to inspire other people around the country to start similar programs at their nearest animal shelter.

The world of dog rescue can take an emotional toll on the people who live it every day. For all the happy endings that replenish the heart and soul, there are just as many heartbreaking endings. Together we can change that. Together we can deliver happily-ever-afters to all animals. What they require is simple: love and care. That's it.

Success of animal rescue requires an entire community. Whether your part is small or large, I encourage you to participate. Everyone has the power to be a hero to an animal in need.

Be a hero, like Judy, my friend Julie's mom. Their family grew up with a home full of animals, and the four-legged creatures still reign the household. Most recently, Judy adopted sibling Poodle-Terrier mixes, Duke and Daisy, from Forgotten Angels Rescue. This organization pulled the puppies from high-kill Lancaster Animal Care Center, located in Los Angeles county.

Be a hero, like my friend Jennifer, who responsibly re-homed her beloved Pug, Samson. Sometimes, life takes a turn that forces us to make tough choices. As much as Jennifer loved Samson, she could not give him the attention and care he deserved. Instead of taking her eight-year old Love Pug to the shelter, she reached out to friends and family to find him the perfect home. That new forever home happened to be with my brother, his wife, their two boys, and their pugalicious Pug, Elly. Samson never had to step paw in a shelter. He went from one happy home to another.

Be a hero, like my friend Noushin and her mom, who rescued a three-week old kitten from the middle of a busy road. One of the kitten's eyes was hanging from its socket, and the other had just burst. In addition to being blind, they soon learned that Joojoo had no teeth and was epileptic. Eight years later, she is living a lavish lifestyle. Joojoo is so spoiled that she only eats *freshly* cooked salmon or chicken. Day-old cuts won't do for this pleasingly plump and picky gal.

Be a hero, like my friend, Karina, who opened her heart and her mind to adopt an abused Staffordshire Bull Terrier from Karma Rescue of Los Angeles. Until Sofie, she believed the selective press surrounding Pit Bulls. When this woman with three kids chose to let go of the negative stigma, she and her Bichon Frise, Jack, met and fell in love with sweet Sofie.

Not only was Sofie used for breeding, but she also had her tongue savagely cut out before being dumped at East Valley Animal Shelter in Los Angeles. She had every reason to hate, but showed nothing except love and gratitude to Karina, who beams with pride when she talks about her beloved family member, "It was Sofie who decided I needed her. You see, Sofie came into my life with a few needs that, as much work as it may sound, it has been nothing compared to what I've already received from her. She reminds me every day that, for the little bit I do, I will receive the kind of unconditional love that only a soul that has been tried can give. Every day she asks for hugs, she wags her tail, and gives the biggest smile when I get home. She lives to make me happy.

"When someone says how wonderful I am to have opened up my home, given her a family of siblings, aunts, uncles, cousins and grandparents, I can only say, 'tell me she hasn't made me better than I was.'"

Be a hero, like Danielle, the hairdresser I met in Bakersfield. She rescued a 4-month-old German Shepherd puppy trapped in a dumpster with a padlock on it. She could not ignore the whimpering she heard as she passed by, so she rushed home to get a bolt cutter. After she saved the young pup from entrapment, she did all the right things: had him scanned for a microchip, reported him missing at the local shelters—providing a photo and her contact information—and, took him to the vet for a health check and shots. Three weeks went by and no one claimed him. Chief is thriving and happy. He follows Danielle everywhere she goes.

Be a hero, like the mom of a gentleman I met during a ride to the airport. She was vacationing along a river in North Carolina. There was a nearby bridge that people would throw unwanted puppies over in an effort to drown them in the rough river waters below it. Most did not make it. One did. He became enamored by this vacationing woman and followed her everywhere during her week-long stay. When the time arrived for her to leave, she was torn. She did not want to leave him behind, but she had a flight home to catch. During the flight, the dog never left her mind. When she arrived home, she called the forest ranger. Sure enough, the dog was sitting and waiting for her outside the cabin where she stayed. She immediately made arrangements to get him to her, giving the loyal dog a forever home.

Be a hero, like Wendy in Massachusetts, who adopted a Chihuahua, Peanut. He was found in the trash in North Carolina with crippled front legs. Thanks to the networking efforts of Eagle's Den Rescue and Toni Diamond Rescue, Peanut found the perfect home with Wendy. She had just lost her beloved Chihuahua, Lexi Loo, who was also disabled. Wendy reached out to Toni saying, "My Lexi Loo passed... if you come across another disabled dog, bring it home for me please. I want to give it a good home. Another disabled dog is the only thing to fill that empty space in my heart. I'm devastated , but Lexi would want another baby to have her warm bed ...And her cart...And her ramps."

Be a hero, like the stranger that I connected with through social media in her desperate efforts to help a friend find her lost dog. This person understood the love and loyalty of a dog because she had one of her own that she rescued off the streets. The dog she saved was a starved, dehydrated Red Nose Pit Bull, who showed clear signs of abuse. In numerous attempts to reunite her with her human, she walked the area with the dog for months knocking on doors. The woman decided that the submissive dog was better off in her care with a full food bowl, full reign over her bed, and a home where she felt safe. Sometimes, bad things happen to good people. The woman became homeless. The only thing that kept her going was the dog she rescued, who had become outgoing and extremely well-mannered in her care. Because of her dog, she could smile when things looked bleak. Because of her dog, she had a warm pillow on cold nights. Because of her dog, she survived being homeless. When you rescue a dog, they rescue you right back.

You can be a hero, too.

Go. Be a hero.

Anything Is PAWSible.

SOURCES

Chapter 1

Denver Better Business Bureau Business Review. Consumer Complaints. Accessed October 19, 2015. http://www.bbb.org

"A Horrible Hundred - Problem Puppy Mills in the United States." The Humane Society of the United States. May 2013. Accessed October 19, 2015. http://www.humanesociety.org

"The AKC: Worst in Show." The Humane Society of the United States. February 6, 2015. Accessed October 19, 2015. http://www.humanesociety.org

CollegeHumor. "The Bizarre Truth About Purebred Dogs (and Why Mutts Are Better) - Adam Ruins Everything." https://www.youtube.com. July 14, 2014. Accessed October 19, 2015.

Allan, Carrie. "The Purebred Paradox." The Human Society of the United States. May 20, 2010. Accessed October 19, 2015. http://www.humanesociety.org.

"Why You Should Spay/Neuter Your Pet." The Humane Society of the United States. August 24, 2014. Accessed October 19, 2015. http://www.humanesociety.org.

Chapter 5

"An Overview of Canine Distemper." Baker Institute : Animal Health : Canine Distemper. Accessed October 20, 2015. http://bakerinstitute.vet.cornell.edu/animalhealth.

Alling, Meredith. "The Facts on Canine Distemper." PetCareRx. November 14, 2013. Accessed October 20, 2015. http://www.petcarerx.com.

Chapter 13

"Robeson County 768 KB.WMV." YouTube. February 5, 2010. Accessed October 23, 2015. https://www.youtube.com.

"The Most Extreme Cruelty - How Shelters Kill Our Best Friends." K9Nation International. Accessed October 23, 2015. http://k9nation.org/killling/howshelterskill.html.

Monahan, Steven. "The Truth About Heart Stick Animal Killing In America's Shelters." Pro Life Animal. September 30, 2013. Accessed October 23, 2015. https://prolifeanimal.wordpress.com.

Bertrand, Joy. "Letter to Robeson County's County Manager -- Sent Tonight." Facebook. March 6, 2010. Accessed October 23, 2015. https://www.facebook.com.

Seiça, Cristina. "Actions For Animals." Animal Shelter Cruel and Horrific Killings. March 7, 2010. Accessed October 23, 2015. http://actionsforanimals.blogspot.com.

Gwynn, Michele. "Robeson County Animal Shelter Walk of Shame Continues!" Examiner.com. June 14, 2010. Accessed October 23, 2015. http://www.examiner.com.

Chapter 20

"EMOTIONAL SUPPORT ANIMALS AND HOUSING." Emotional Support Animal Center. 2014. Accessed October 25, 2015. http://www.emotionalsupportanimalcenter.com.

Einhorn, Dori. "Renting with an Emotional Support Dog, Service Dog or Therapy Dog." Einhorn Insurance Agency. April 9, 2012. Accessed October 26, 2015. http://einhorninsurance.com.

"More Than Just a Pet." Invisible Disabilities Association. Accessed October 26, 2015. http://invisibledisabilities.org.

Chapter 21

"Where to Get Your New Rabbit." The Humane Society of the United States. August 1, 2014. Accessed October 28, 2015. http://www.humanesociety.org.

McVeigh, Tracy. "Pet Rabbits Are Cruelly Neglected and Mistreated in Britain, Survey Finds." The Gaurdian. May 21, 2011. Accessed October 28, 2015. http://www.theguardian.com.

Chapter 23

Serrie, Jonathan. "Pet Euthanasia Rates Decline at US Shelters." Fox News. April 21, 2014. Accessed October 24, 2015. http://www.foxnews.com.

"Statistics & Facts." The Dog Rescuers. 2009. Accessed October 24, 2015. http://www.thedogrescuers.com.

"Animal Shelter Euthanasia." American Humane Association. Accessed October 24, 2015. http://www.americanhumane.org.

"Pet Statistics." ASPCA. Accessed October 24, 2015. https://www.aspca.org.

Burger, James. "Animal Shelter Kill Rates Continue to Rise." The Bakersfield Californian. February 8, 2012. Accessed October 24, 2015. http://www.bakersfield.com.

Farmer, Liz. "When Cities and Counties Fight, Sometimes It's the Animals That Suffer." Governing. December 16, 2013. Accessed October 23, 2015. http://www.governing.com.

"Kern County Animal Control: No Truth to Mass-killing Rumor." BakersfieldNow.com. September 6, 2013. Accessed October 23, 2015. http://www.bakersfieldnow.com.

"Social Media Increasing Pet Adoption Rates." ISYS6621 Social Media for Managers. April 26, 2015. Accessed October 24, 2015. http://isys6621.com.

Dawson, Christopher. "7 Ways to Make an Impact on Homeless Pets." CNN. July 9, 2015. Accessed October 24, 2015. http://www.cnn.com.

Merrill, Elijah. "Social Media Boosts Dog Adoption Efforts." The Dog Daily. 2012. Accessed October 24, 2015. http://www.thedogdaily.com.